Indomitable Ladies

The generosity of these sponsors have made possible the publication of *Indomitable Ladies of the St. Cloud Reading Room Society, 1880-2010*.

For gifts of $100 or more.

Barbara Carlson
LaVaughn Bangston
Mabel Coborn
Karel Helgeson
Drs. Kathleen and H.T. Hobday
Beulah Rose Hutchens
Marilyn and Robert Obermiller
Dr. Barbara Saigo
The Family of A.G. and Alice Whitney
Patricia and Robert Witte

Other contributions were made by members of the St. Cloud Reading Room Society.

This project was funded in part or in whole with money from the vote of the people of Minnesota on November 4, 2008, which dedicated funding to preserve Minnesota's arts and cultural heritage.

Indomitable Ladies

of the St. Cloud Reading Room Society

1880 to 2010

Written by:
Patricia K. Witte

Member of the General Federation of Women's Clubs

Cover photo: The 1897-1898 members of the Reading Room Society meet (on the lawn) of the home of Dr. and Mrs. H. Dunn. From left to right: the Dunns, Mrs. A.H. Reinhard, Mrs. A.L. Tileston, Mrs. H.C. Waite, Mrs. Thomas Foley (with a guest, her niece, behind her), Mrs. Robert Harrison, Mrs. C.A. Gilman, Mrs. A. Barto, Mrs. W.L. Beebe (on the ground in front, Molly Foley), Mrs. H.C. Ervin, Mrs. W.B. Mitchell, Mrs. John Coates (a guest, Mrs Homan, is beind her), Mrs. Alva Eastman, Mrs. J.B. Dunn, and Mrs. Martin Molitor.

Copyright © 2010 Reading Room Society

Printed in the United States of America

ISBN: 978-0-87839-411-1

Published by North Star Press of St. Cloud, Inc.
P.O. Box 451
St. Cloud, Minnesota 56302

Acknowledgements

Many people have participated in the work of compiling this book. The History Book Committee of the Reading Room Society met and kept up to date on my progress, made suggestions and were on call for special needs. Constance Crane, for instance, took the job of indexing the book; Yvonne Schilplin took over responsibilities of getting pictures ready for publication and met with Bobbie Bright, Joan Teigen, and Della Anderson weekly to help with this task. Helen Catton helped with this too. This was especially helpful during a period of three months while I was recuperating from an accident I had in January.

As always, John Decker was most helpful in the museum archives as was Bob Lommel until his retirement. The staff of the History Center is to be praised as well as thanked.

Members of Reading Room have been supportive throughout the two years of this work. And also worthy of praise are the women throughout our one hundred thirty years who have carefully cared for their archives, which now reside at the Stearns History Museum Resource Center. Pictures, minutes, newspaper accounts fill many boxes and albums.

And to my husband, Bob Witte, for his great patience and interest in the progress of the book. He patiently read and re-read these pages to edit and point out inconsistencies and need for re-writes.

Thank you, thank you all.

Pat Witte

Table of Contents

Introduction

When I began to write this book, the story of the Reading Room Society, I was enthralled by the energy of those women who had come from so far away to live and give support to their husbands and raise their families. After a long journey, a journey from home for them, they reached an unknown place where the land was only beginning to be tamed and the building of a town was rough hewn.

The women I write about, at the beginning were not necessarily new to the United States. Many came from Eastern states that had been settled for several generations, and had good schools and refinements of a good life. As I got to know them it was evident that they soon had a vision of what life could be, even in this rough place in the middle of this huge country. I was thrilled by their efforts to bring some of the culture they had known right here with them, and they were able to state their goals to the local establishment that they intended to work for a free library. A goal. And they went for it. This was in 1865.

Twenty-one years they first reached that goal with the beautiful classic Carnegie Library, then on to the library that opened in 1978 after a long period of convincing the voters that the beloved Carnegie

Library was too small and out of date. By 2008, the Great River Library was built and opened. These had been the driving force for the Reading Room Society; now the goal had been reached. The citizens have taken their responsibility for its maintenance; the library had become a state-of-the-art complicated machine with professional people manning it.

Reading Room had to ask, What next? That is what this book is about—it echoes the questions of hundreds, perhaps thousands of service organizations throughout our country whose goals have been reached. Organizations that started when towns were small, just developing in every facet of their lives; few people were educated to professions. Hence, the organizations in which members pulled together to support a cause. Many of these organizations in the last few years have died out. Now What? Some have become sociable societies with a great history to recall. Others, like St. Cloud Reading Room have taken a good look at what they stood for, what they have accomplished and made resolve to move foward into a new time with new calls to service in their community.

The Society is like a new pioneer organization taking baby steps as they look at new problems in their communities that might be calling to them. The end is not here—but a new beginning.

PKW
10/25/2010

CHAPTER ONE

1857: A Community Is Planted

*L*ured by tantalizing advertisements in eastern newspapers that described good farm land, rich forests and grand new settlements on the Mississippi River, the first settlers in St. Cloud streamed in from Eastern states in the mid 1850s. There was great promise, even for those who came with very little, and great increase for those with money to speculate.

People from the northeastern states who spoke English and settled in Lower Town, built their Presbyterian, Methodist and Episcopalian churches, and Unitarian as well as a Friends meeting house. They were determined to organize a society as they knew it in the old settled

Those who came by boat in the 1860s were greeted by this view of St. Cloud. This community would have been to the left going up river. (Photo courtesy Stearns History Museum)

St. Cloud in the early 1860s. (Photo courtesy Stearns History Museum)

states of New England and New York. Lower Town was that area south of the ravine, along the river, and west to Lake George. It would be the site of the St. Cloud Normal School before the century ended. Among the residents were teachers, lawyers, and other professional people, as well as business people.

The largest group of immigrants were Germans from Bavaria new to the ways of life in the United States. Their foreign language was an impediment, and their different customs and religion set them apart from the Yankees who preceded them. They were Roman Catholics who built a wood church in 1857 to serve their religious needs, their social life and school. They settled in Middle Town, along what would become St. Germain Street. By 1864 they had built a brick Gothic-style church on St. Germain. This was the area north of the ravine that ran to the river from Lake George and south of the North Fifth Street ravine. Most of the very early settlers of this group were tradesmen and shopkeepers, followed by farmers who would till the land and mill the grain.

Another group of pioneers moved in from the south to settle Upper Town, building plantation-style homes. They even brought their slaves. But most of them departed after the start of the Civil War, or after having experienced a Minnesota winter. Upper Town is described as that area east of the river from where the hospital now stands.

These first settlements took place during 1853 to 1855. Finally, they merged to become the town of St. Cloud in 1856. And that was two years before Minnesota received statehood in 1858. Settling into this rugged place, the women from the Eastern states must have looked longingly to the refinements of their sisters back home. The German Catholic women had their own society and big families, similar to life in their homeland—German music, art, food, their church, and their language and stories.

A Cultural Life Is Planted on the Frontier.

The desire for books and an eagerness to fashion a cultural life in their new surroundings prompted a group of eight women to form a Library Association. They were women who were educated in Eastern women's institutes and "finishing schools." Theirs was certainly nothing like the education women have known in more recent years, but they were accustomed to the arts, literature, and philosophy as they were taught in their former environment. They brought with them an ideal of what life should become even in this prairie enclave on the upper Mississippi River.

On June 8, 1865, an article in the *St. Cloud Democrat* reported that at the home of Mrs. L.H. Morse, eight Lower Town women met and formed a Library Association which would meet on alternate Thursdays. Officers were elected at that first meeting: president, Mrs. Charles Bridgeman; vice-president, Mrs. L. Cramb; secretary, Minnie Moe; and treasurer, Mrs. C.N. Mason. The very early membership soon swelled to sixty men and women. Dues were set at ten cents per meeting and would be used to purchase books. As they progressed, the women met in the afternoons at members' homes and were joined by the men at the end of their work day for supper. After the meal, members read from books or gave prepared talks, sometimes musical performances.

St. Germain Street and Fifth Avenue, the Joseph Edelbrock Building was the site of the Post Office on the first floor and the first free public library was on the second. (Photo courtesy Stearns History Museum)

They were encouraged when an item in the *Democrat* gave news that General C.A. Andrews would present one hundred dollars to the Association to purchase new books if that same amount could be raised by the members. The newspaper announced the following week: "The ladies of the Library Association will give a dinner next week at the Court House to raise the money." One hundred fifteen dollars were raised. General Christopher C. Andrews was a Lower Town resident and a lawyer. He was sent a collection of books from Edward Everette for whom the first school was named. The books, according to John Dominik, "became the nucleus for the town library." (John Dominik, *St. Cloud, the Triplet City.*" 1983 Windsor Publications.)

By 1867, the Library Association had seventy-eight books. With General Andrews's contribution and money raised at the supper, one hundred new books were added. The women took turns as librarian and the books were moved in turn to homes of the members. However, the Library Association women had great hope for a central reading room in a public place.

But hopes were impeded by differences of opinion between two factions that grew within the Association. The friction arose between those who felt the need for enlarging membership in the Library Association and those who wished to keep the social suppers exclusive. A larger membership would of course mean more dues, but social aspects of the organization had become important to the second group. The quarrel between the two factions resulted in their meeting separately, one actually drawing up articles of incorporation and electing officers, the other holding onto books in its possession and electing its own officers. Finally, a committee of members representing both groups met to resolve their differences. It was reported in the *St. Cloud Journal*:

"The committee from the two factions of the Library Association met on Tuesday, July second, and arranged a plan for reuniting the two." The plan was to incorporate as the Union Library Association, and in December 1872, thirty-seven signers were listed.

The *St. Cloud Journal* reported: "Virtuoso! St. Cloud has an excellent library for a town of its size and one that is eminently worthy of more support than it receives. There are 840 volumes in the book collection which, in the seven years of our library history, have had 3,673 issues (dating from 1865). Two hundred borrowers have been registered."

As disagreements were settled between the two sides in the disputes, followed by dropping the social activities, in 1873, there began a period when the library was "boarded out" among stores in the business district. This continued until 1878 when Hall's Book Store, which had been the first such location, had a business decline and the library had to be moved. The books were moved to the City Clerk's office to be available two afternoons a week, and could be rented by non-members of the Association for ten cents a day. This was followed in 1879 by a campaign for new members. The newspaper urged "every family of average intelligence to join." The Union Library Association, both

Mrs. Helen Moore's house where, in 1880, forty-four women met and organized the Reading Room Society. (Photo courtesy Reading Room Society Archives)

factions, were able to work together for a short time for the purpose of obtaining a free central reading room for St. Cloud. They also resumed the social activities of the early Library Association.

THE PLANTING TAKES ROOT . . .
THE READING ROOM SOCIETY, 1880

THE UNION LIBRARY ASSOCIATION was not a satisfactory solution in the opinion of many of the members. Their goal as early as 1867, was to provide a free library and also a reading room. On February 12, 1880, forty-four members of the original Library Association met to discuss the possibility of securing a free public reading room for St. Cloud. It was here at Mrs. Helen Moore's house that the St. Cloud Reading Room Society was born. That day they adopted a constitution. The new Society was exclusively composed of pioneer women in a library movement with a constitution with a stated purpose of the establishment and maintenance of a free reading room in the City of

Mrs. H.C. Waite (Maria Clark) was elected first president of the Reading Room Society in 1880. (Photo courtesy Stearns History Museum)

St. Cloud. This goal was to be accompanied by the promotion of literary and social culture. The constitution was read and adopted, and the following officers were elected: President, Mrs. H.C. Waite; vice-president, Mrs. W.B. Mitchell; secretary Mrs. L.W. Collins, and treasurer, Mrs. P. Tenney.

The following forty-four women were members the first year of the Society's existence. The Mesdames H.C. Waite*, W.B. Mitchell*, P. Tenney*, D.B. Searle, H.P. Bennett, D.S. Hayward, J.G. Smith, E.D. Moore, Lewis Clark, M.J. Whitman, L.H. Morse**, L.A. Marlatt, the Misses Isabel Lawrence, C. Lawrence*, Inez Moore, J. Owen, A.B. Crommette, M.L. Upham, the Mesdames S.E. Wing, M.B.S. Barnes, Helen M. Moore*, S.E. Tolman, P.L. Gregory, C.L. Schulten, L.W. Collins, N.P. Clarke*, M.S. Hayward, L.A. Evans, William Barrette, W.W. Wright, J. Cooper, E.A. Parks, W.L. Beebe*, C. McClure, C.A. Gilman, C.H. Hines, C.S. Benson, J.E. West, C.F. Lewis, D.H. Freeman*, J.F. Stevenson*, D.M.G. Murphy, G.H. Davis, and John Coates*.(Names with asterisks indicate charter members.) Two years later, in 1882, the Reading Room Society was incorporated. Some 125 years later an application for tax exempt status was made and accepted.

Mrs. L.H. Morse had been one of the eight women who had, in 1865, gone to the town officials to declare the intention of working for reading room and library.)

A law was passed by the state legislature in 1879 that provided: "That the City Council of an incorporated city, or village Council of any incorporated village, shall have power to establish and maintain a public library and reading room, for the use and benefit of the inhabitants of such city or village, and may levy a tax, not to exceed one mill on the dollar annually, and in cities of over thirty thousand inhabitants, not to exceed one-half mill on the dollar annually, on all the taxable property in the city, such tax to be levied and collected in like manner with other general taxes of said city or village to be known as the 'Library Fund.'"

The *St. Cloud Journal Press* reported on March 16, 1882: "At its meeting March 9, the Library Association appointed a committee consisting of Messrs. Spencer, Tolman, and Searles, to present to the City Council a proposition to accept as a 'gift to the city the library and to maintain it.'" This was called for in the general law of the state, to be known as the "St. Cloud Public Library."

By May 11, it was reported that the library of the St. Cloud Library Association had been tendered to the City Council, but nobody had taken any action in the matter. In fact, the books were piled up in the hallway leading to the Masonic lodge room, which was located in the same building.

St. Cloud City Council adopted a resolution: "That a public library under the provisions of the general law of the state, be established to be known as the St. Cloud Public Library."

The City Council accepted the books offered by the Library Association. The tax of 1884 provided for the support of the library the sum of five hundred dollars. The Library Association had elected its own board of directors. The law of 1879 required that a new library board be appointed by the mayor having nine directors. The first board of directors of the St. Cloud Public Library—all men—consisted of: L.C. Collins, G.S. Spencer, Bernard Reinhart, J.E. West, Grant Tolman, Theodore Bruener, N.F. Barnes, P.B. Gorman, and H.J. Rosenberger. On May 11, 1883, the directors of the Library Association met to turn their library over to the new city board and then the Library Association adjourned for good. Many of its members were also members of the Reading Room Society. The new city library board organized immediately and elected as its first president, Captain J.E. West, a member of the Library Association from 1865 until its end. Mr. Barnes was appointed the first librarian of the St. Cloud Public Library.

The book collection turned over to the new organization included one thousand volumes, but two hundred were in dilapidated condition. There were 139 registered borrowers, and the circulation for the year was 1,371 .

Mr. G.S. Spencer, who also had been an active member of the Library Association, was appointed librarian in 1886, following Mr. Barnes, another member of the Association. Mr. Spencer moved the library books into the room above his store in the Edelbrock Building.

The City of St. Cloud now had a public library in the Edelbrock Building, a general store on the corner of Fifth Avenue and St.Germain Street.

But the pioneer dream of a free reading room had still not been realized. In March 1886, the Reading Room Society offered to contribute three hundred dollars a year toward the project of a "Union Reading Room and City Library."

The *St. Cloud Journal Press* editorialized: "The services of a lady librarian to take charge of the reading room and library will be at least three hundred dollars a year. Periodicals will cost approximately one hundred dollars; desirable quarters may be secured for one hundred and fifty dollars a year, but it will cost about two hundred dollars to fix up the rooms. The city now contributed five hundred dollars to the support of the city library which, combined with the proffered three hundred dollars of the Reading Room Society, will make eight hundred dollars. After meeting the above expenses, there will be not more than one hundred dollars left for the purchase of books, for rebinding, for heat and gas and upkeep. We feel thousands of citizens would heartily endorse the project, but in the present state of affairs it does not seem possible that it will be accomplished."

But the editor was wrong. He had not recognized the business acumen of these women. And, so too the city fathers who found the proposition "inexpedient at this time." The business expertise of the women was remarkable and often commended by the other newspapers of the time. Yes, they were, many of them, of good economic standing, although it was not personal wealth they relied on for Reading Room activities. They worked on money-raising projects—from art exhibits and concerts to rummage sales. From the very first day, they agreed to refrain from spending capital. When their offer was turned down, they placed the club's one thousand one hundred dollars in the bank, which paid as much as ten percent interest. It became their fund and it would grow for providing the reading room of the future.

With this investment the standing committee was created, with Mrs. L. W. Collins, Chairman. Later, the funds were invested in shares with the St. Cloud Building Association.

By May, the Reading Room Society had raised one hundred and twenty-five dollars to pay a year's rent in advance on the room in the Edelbrock building. The Society also undertook to furnish the room, which was about twenty by thirty-five feet in size. In July 1886, the free public reading room was opened for the circulation of books and to furnish a spot where anyone might indulge in leisurely reading. The hours were 1:30 to 5:45 and from 7:00 to 9:00 p.m. each day. The birth of the St. Cloud Library had taken place after a long labor. And with the improved facility, Mr. G.S. Spencer continued as librarian.

For several years, the Reading Room Society supported the combination public library and reading room. Beside the three hundred dollar annual contribution and the payment of the rent, it purchased the necessary items for maintaining the physical needs of the rooms, such necessities as payment for a person to clean the space, a wood box, broom and dust pan, for stereoptican views, and more. They spent seventy-five dollars for a desk and tables, and successfully raised money through concerts, lectures, social gatherings, bazaars, and rummage sales. The Society publicized the reading room, inviting everyone to use it with signs posted in boarding houses, hotels, saloons, grocery stores, and other public places around town.

Minutes of June 2, 1892: "The matter of cleaning the Reading Room was called up, but was left entirely to the Reading Room committee." Everyday matters were handled by the Society.

"On motion of Mrs Mitchell it was voted to close the Reading Room on Sunday evenings during the months of June, July, and August." June 30 minutes reported, "that the Reading Room had been cleaned at a cost of $5.00."

During the first seven years of the library, the book collection grew from about twelve hundred volumes to twenty-five hundred and ten volumes. But alas, within a few years, the first library-reading room in the Edelbrock Building had become too small. A move had to be made.

1890 TO 1897

THE SOCIETY FOUND TIME FOR INTELLECTUAL GROWTH AS WELL.

IN THE YEAR 1890, MINUTES reflect the weekly meetings of the early society and the continuous rapid growth of membership with one or two new members "admitted to membership" each week. Then, in October 1890, the minutes state, "the membership of the Society shall be limited to sixty." When put to a vote, it was adopted unanimously. By 1891, it was reported that, "the year opened with forty members and during the year eight new members were added, but through the consequence of removal, there are today only thirty-eight."

"Twenty-four meetings have been held with an average attendance of twenty-two and-a-half . . ."

While the Reading Room was growing according to the original plan to provide a library in the city, it was also fulfilling another of its goals: The stated goal of the Society would be better served if they made plans to improve their intellectual growth. They started out by having weekly meetings with readings on subjects ranging from dress reform to Woman's Suffrage in the first few years. By 1887, they began to have many original papers presented by men and women of St. Cloud who were expert in subjects of interest to them.

In 1897, the first Program Committee was appointed. With this committee, new courses of study were introduced. The study courses included Sociology, the English Novel, Italian Art, Writers of Today, Nature Study, Great Industries of Our Age, Famous Women, Literary Pilgrimage through the British Isles, Minnesota, Study of Magazine Articles, Drama, and Opera. Each course was divided into a year of programs.

Lecture courses, concert recitals, art exhibits were encouraged and many were programmed for the public under the auspices of Reading Room Society.

They began working toward a larger, permanent location:

TO: Common Council of the City of St. Cloud: "We, the undersigned, were appointed a committee by the St. Cloud Reading Room Society to represent to your honorable body the following facts concerning the City Library and to ask you for an adequate appropriation for the maintenance of the same.

"At the present time the Reading Room and Library occupy the same room, which is not large enough to accommodate either, and is poorly lighted. It is proposed to move the library to new quarters that will allow a separate room for library and reading room.

"Books of high order, including the best references, are constantly called for. This is an encouraging indication of the intellectual character of our people and their interest in the best things; but the library is not prepared to meet the demand made upon it. This fact does much to check a growing interest in reading and study, as a taste for scholarship grows by what it feeds upon. We are very confident that your high appreciation of such a disposition on the part of the people, especially the younger generation, will make it a pleasure for you to provide the means of developing it.

"To increase the efficiency of the library by the addition of the necessary books and by locating in more desirable quarters will require an addition to present resources. A half mil tax upon the city valuation would meet these needs and we respectfully petition your honorable body to levy such a tax."

Signed: Mrs. Joseph Carhart, Mrs. L.A. Cramb, Mrs. C.A. Gilman, Mrs. Charlotte A. Barto, Mrs. Frank E. Searle."

As the library developed, the City Council had created a Library Board to oversee the city's interest in the Library. So, at this point, there was some discussion as to why the cost estimates were being given to them by the Reading Room Society rather than the Library Board. But

West Hotel, 1895. Location of the free Reading Room and Library opening in 1896 by the Reading Room Society. (Photo courtesy Stearns History Museum)

the City Council decided to vote eight hundred dollars to support the library for 1894. A few days later the Library Board held a special meeting to consider the proposed location in the West Hotel, on the corner of Fifth Avenue and First Street South, and approved it.

Early in 1894 the library was moved into three spacious rooms in the West Hotel. Instead of one room to provide all the services, there were now rooms for the librarian's office, a reading room with newspapers and periodicals, and another with shelving for the books. In 1894, Mrs. Marie E. Brick became librarian. A catalog of books was compiled and the library was open from 1:30 to 5:30 and from 7:00 to 9:00 p.m. daily, and the St. Cloud community must certainly have been proud and pleased with its fine new library. For seven years, the library served the community in the comfortable and attractive rooms in the West Hotel.

But then, disaster struck. On February 8, 1901, the West Hotel burned to the ground and all of the library's records and most of the books were consumed by the fire.

One of three spacious rooms in the West Hotel lobby. (Photo courtesy Stearns History Museum)

CHAPTER TWO

A Free Library for All the People of St. Cloud

HELP SOUGHT FROM PHILANTHROPIST ANDREW CARNEGIE FOR A NEW BUILDING

Two years before the disaster, the Reading Room had read the words of the great philanthropist, Andrew Carnegie, a statement in which he "found nothing promising such large returns as cooperation with communities willing to pledge themselves permanently to devote from public funds, for the annual maintenance of a public library, one tenth the sum given by him for a building." Basing hope in Mr. Carnegie's words two years before, in 1899, the Reading Room sent him a letter asking for funds, but with no results. (Taken from *Profile of a Library*, a paper by Mrs. Tom Donlin on the history of Reading Room, circa 1960.)

A day after the fire, however, in 1901, Mr. Alvah Eastman, husband of the Society president, wrote a letter requesting once again a grant for a library building. Mr. Eastman received an immediate reply from Mr. Carnegie, which stated that he would award twenty-five thousand dollars to St. Cloud for a library building if the city would furnish the site and promise at least twenty-five hundred dollars annually for maintenance. The indomitable ladies of the Reading

Room Society at once asked the city for the privilege of donating the land for the library building. The city accepted the Society's offer and picked two lots, located on the corner of Fifth Avenue and Second Street, which could be purchased for five thousand dollars. But another hurdle appeared when the Library Board was indignant that the Reading Room Society had assumed the Library Board's function by presenting the offer of the site for the Carnegie Library to the board. However, the board had not been notified of Mr. Carnegie's monetary offer and tabled any action. The dispute between the City Council and Library Board was solved when members of both sides recognized that jurisdiction as to decision of site and erection of the library building properly belonged to the Library Board. But the services and influence of the Society were still needed.

Mrs. W.B. Mitchell, a Reading Room member, solicited James J. Hill, "Empire Builder," who contributed two thousand dollars toward the site purchase. Citizens contributed almost a thousand dollars. Reading Room members, who had time and again proven themselves excellent fund raisers, raised the remainder. On February 17, 1901, the Reading Room Society authorized its committee to purchase the site and give to the City Council "a good and sufficient warranty deed which shall specify that said tract of land shall be used for library purposes only and upon its failure to be so used it shall go back to the Reading Room Society." The City Council accepted gratefully. Later in the spring they sent the following letter to the Society:

"Reading Room Society, St. Cloud, Minnesota

"The Common Council of the City of St. Cloud extends a vote of thanks to the Reading Room Society in appreciation of its munificent gift to the city of a site for new library building, testifying to your enterprise and interest in the welfare and progress of our city."

The West Hotel fire occurred on February 8, 1901. In the next nineteen days Andrew Carnegie had been contacted and had offered his gift with certain stipulations. The City Council had agreed to meet these stipulations. The Reading Room Society had found a site, and found financing for the site, had offered it to the City Council and important problems of governmental jurisdiction had been settled. Prime movers behind all these rapid events stood the members of the Reading Room Society in good stead.

The Society cooperated with other organizations to benefit the new library. A "minstrel show" drew good audiences at the Davidson Theatre. It was sponsored by the Elk's Lodge and the Reading Room Society. A total of $760 was raised to be divided between the two organizations.

"A fine entertainment" brought congratulations to the Society and the Schumann Club in a cooperative venture: a presentation of music by local vocalist, Miss Willis and the high school orchestra. "The stage was artistically decorated. In its adornment were used potted plants, palm, ferns, roses, carnations, oriental rugs, couches, pillows, etc. Its arrangement was a credit to the taste of the ladies and benefit to the library" (*St. Cloud Journal Press*). Plans for the building were submitted by three architects. The plan selected was a classic style building with a central entrance, set back forty-five feet from the sidewalk line on Fifth Avenue and thirty feet back on Second Street South. The architects chosen were from the architectural firm of Patton, Fisher, and Miller of Chicago. Construction began.

READING ROOM THANKED FOR GIFT OF LAND.
SOCIETY PROMISES ASSISTANCE IN THE FUTURE.

IN DECEMBER THE LIBRARY BOARD sent the following letter:

Mrs. Alvah Eastman, President
Ladies Reading Room Society
St. Cloud, Minn., December 7, 1901

Dear Madam:

By unanimous consent of the St. Cloud Public Library Board I am instructed to convey to your society the thanks of said Board for your generous gift of three lots on which the new Public Library is now in course of erection. The Board greatly appreciates the public spirit which has been shown by your society through its long years of labor in behalf of the Public Library, and hopes to be able to complete at an early date a building upon these lots, that will be a credit alike to the city, to your own society and to itself.

By Order of the Board, H.C. Irvin, Secretary

Alice Eastman (Mrs. Alvah) was president of Reading Room during the time of building and opening the new library. (Photo courtesy of the Stearns History Museum)

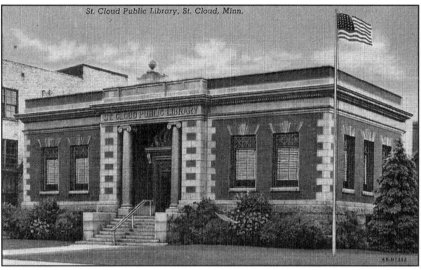

St. Cloud Public Library, St. Cloud, Minn.

Andrew Carnegie provided $25,000 to build a library. The Carnegie Library opened in 1902. (Photo courtesy of the Stearns History Museum)

On December 9, Mrs. Molitor offered to the board a Reading Room Society resolution: "Resolved that the Ladies Reading Room Society signify to the Library Board, that the Reading Room Society stands ready to assist the Library Board and that it is ready to consider any requests that the Board may make."

The board quickly responded with a request for the Society to furnish four columns, either polished granite or oak to use in the main room, or complete the auditorium in the basement or to do both "if they so desire."

A letter from C.F. MacDonald, president of the Library Board: "I have the honor to acknowledge the receipt of your letter of the 21st inst. advising the Public Library Board that your society had guaranteed to provide four polished granite columns to take the place of the proposed ones in adamant.

"All things considered, we have made as good progress as could reasonably be expected, indeed much better than any other 'Carnegie Library' building of which is knowledge. It is already assured that St. Cloud is to have a public library building which will be an ornament to the city, and of great and lasting benefit to its people."

In 1902, the total number of books in the St. Cloud Library were 5,883. The principal classifications were: General Works, Reference, Travel and Description, Bound Periodicals, History, Philosophy, Biography, Religion, Fiction, Sociology, German Books, Language, U.S. Documents, Natural Sciences, State Documents, Useful Arts, Fine Arts, and Literature.

Andrew Carnegie. (Photo in the public domain.)

The four granite columns with ionic capitals, costing five hundred and five dollars, were given to the library by the Society

Four polished granite columns in the main room of the library. They now stand in Court House Square downtown St. Cloud. The furnishings were also a gift of the Reading Room Society. (Photo courtesy Stearns History Museum)

in honor of its twenty-first anniversary. These were used in the center hall of the interior. At an April 1902 meeting, the Board accepted the offer of a brass tablet made by Mr. L.W. Collins. It was to be erected above the main entrance door of the library and to be engraved: "This tablet is inscribed to Andrew Carnegie, through whose generosity this building has been erected upon a site donated by the Ladies Reading Room Society 1902." Those columns were eventually moved to the County Court House Plaza, where they now stand.

The board, at their August 1 meeting, determined that they were running over budget on the twenty-five thousand dollar gift from Mr. Carnegie, and, therefore, named a committee to request the Reading Room Society to buy chairs and tables for the two reading rooms in the library. The Society agreed to this six-hundred-dollar expense for "six tables, 13 feet long as per the architects' plans, and 60 chairs."

On September 10, 1901, at twenty-one years (counting from 1880), the Reading Room Society reported a full membership of sixty ladies, the maximum stipulated by the by-laws.

A BRILLIANT SUCCESS!

THE TWENTY-FIRST ANNIVERSARY of the Reading Room Society was observed on February 22, 1901 (George Washington's birthday), to celebrate their "coming of age" and the brilliant success of the past in those few years. All sixty members of the Society were present with their husbands who were duly thanked for their contributions to their luminous history, especially the building and opening of the Carnegie Library, which was about to begin. The celebration took place at the Unity church parlors. Mrs. Eastman presided.

After delivering a short history of Reading Room for its first twenty-one years, Mrs. G.W. Stewart spoke on the subject of "The Husbands of the Reading Room," and her clever toast was in part as follows:

"You will pardon I hope, gentlemen, any undue levity or exhibition of exuberance of spirit on the part of the assembled, but we naturally feel somewhat elated over the recent good fortune which has come upon us all. I refer to the favorable though somewhat tardy reply that has been received by you to the letter our society wrote to Mr. Carnegie somewhat over a year and a half ago. And then we feel great pleasure in having you with us this evening." This, in reference to the

Emily Mitchell poured tea at a "coming of age" party in 1901, the Society's 21st year. (Photo courtesy Stearns History Museum)

A celebration at the Davidson Theatre with the Elks Club raised $760.00 for the new library. The Davidson no longer stands. (Photo courtesy Stearns History Museum)

letter sent to Carnegie by Alvah Eastman, which was given immediate reply.

The place was aptly decorated in red, white, and blue and the "progressive tea" of three courses was served splendidly Then, following the tea was a program of toasts, "crisp, inspiring, stimulating," and a musical program. In addition, Captain J.E. West spoke of the Beginning of St. Cloud and of the library. He gave a short history of the early settlement, which was to be published in the near future.

Mrs. W.B. Mitchell, the first vice-president of the Society, spoke: "The Reading Room Society is almost old enough to speak for itself, and we hope that in all these twenty-one years it has spoken for itself, in fostering that which is elevating and improving in the community." She recalled the meeting at Helen Moore's house when they organized a society for the purpose of advancing the interests of our city library and establishing a free reading room.

"In addition to this purpose there was a desire to promote sociability in our little town and to break up church cliques and broaden our interests. In March 1882, having by dues and entertainments collected several hundred dollars, the 'real estate fever' took possession of us, and since to own property we must be an incorporated body, we took the necessary steps to become incorporated. At this time a very desirable lot was on the market, the one on which stood the old post office building, recently destroyed by fire. The owner was an apparently innocent young man who, when visited by a committee of ladies, fixed the price of his property at $600. The offer was accepted, and the committee authorized to close the purchase at once. When the ladies again visited him, not an hour after the action had been taken by the Society with money to make payment, they discovered to their intense surprise that through some unknown influence he had experienced a change of mind and demanded $800, a price in excess of the value of the lot and of our means. While the minutes record the report of the committee, there is no official record of the intense disappointment that was felt over the failure of the negotiations, through 'fribbleness' of the 'not-so-innocent-as-he-looked young man.'

"That is as near as Reading Room has ever come to buying property, although the matter has many times been agitated and discussed with much enthusiasm. Some of us hope before another year has passed to have our minutes chronicle the fact that we have bought a lot and that Mr. Carnegie's very generous gift rests upon it.

"Of the charter members, all but five have belonged to the Society continuously. They have seen many ups and downs, have had many heart aches over the loss of valuable members by death and by removal from town, have listened to and taken part in many heated discussions, have been united and divided in opinions, have suffered the injustice, even of being called 'old ladies' and perhaps have been slow to see that frequent allusions to the past energy and self-sacrifice was not always entertaining to new members, but through it all there has been a spirit of good nature and kindliness and a long, strong pull together for what we wanted, to advance the best interests of the library and reading room."

She went on to discuss the library and reading room in the West Hotel and report that Reading Room had spent $3,950 toward this pet project, beside many purchases made for comforts and conveniences. Now, in 1901 they were "on the verge of seeing the full fruition of our fondest hopes and can confidently look forward to the erection of an elegant home for our library and reading room, including, we hope, a club for our Society in which a year hence it may be possible to entertain our gentlemen friends at our second 'progressive tea.'" (It appears that there were hopes that there would be a space in the new library-to-be where the Reading Room might meet.)

THE PROGRAM COMMITTEE FOR THE YEAR 1902 announced a program of nature study. The treasurer reported $434 collected, dues and fees, for the year; $600 had been drawn from their stock in the building and loan association to purchase books, tables, and chairs for the library, the balance in the treasury, $78.00. The present value of stock investments, about $1,500. The election of officers took place on September 11, 1903. (At that time, more frequently the years are counted from the date of incorporation, 1882, but not consistently.)

The officers in 1903 were Mrs. Mrs. C.A. Cooper, president; Mrs. Frederick Schilplin, secretary; and Mrs. W.B. Mitchell, treasurer.

Highlight of 1904 was the Juried State Arts Exhibit by the Minnesota State Arts Society, April 4 to 16. The Exhibition Committee of the State Arts Board conferred with the committee of the Reading Room Society to make arrangements for the exhibit to be held at the Carnegie Library. Artwork from the galleries of T.B. Walker of Minneapolis and James J. Hill, St. Paul, were among the items to be shown. This was a "first" for St. Cloud. It was offered free to the public. Paintings, sculpture, drawings, carvings, architectural designs, textile fabrics and all art craft media were exhibited. Beside numerous entries from different parts of Minnesota, the Art Society received contributions from Boston, New York, Santa Barbara, California, and more. It was a juried show, with a committee of judges consisting of Robert Koehler and Ernest Kennedy of Minneapolis, and Miss Julia Gautier of St. Paul. Lectures on art were given at the exhibition and informal talks by art connoisseurs of Minnesota. It was a notable event in art circles across the country. "It will show our sisters of the Atlantic that we have a few microbes of culture ourselves" (*Journal Press,* March 11, 1904). The Reading Room members organized the exhibit for the library and acted as hostesses for the welcoming and other events of the affair.

In the following year, the Reading Room Society observed its silver anniversary by asking past and present members to contribute silver dollars. Two hundred eighty-four dollars were received. Members and guests enjoyed a Progressive Tea in the Unity Church Parlors, to which the husbands were also invited. The Society had purchased four Arundel prints and one photogravure for the silver dollars as a gift to the library to enhance its décor . . . and to commemorate the thirtieth anniversary of the Reading Room in 1910. The *St. Cloud Daily Times* story noted: "A brilliant gathering of ladies and gentlemen attended an exquisitely appointed banquet and charming musical to mark the thirtieth anniversary of the St. Cloud Ladies Reading Room Society. The event was given Saturday evening at the handsome home of Mrs. A.L. Riley on Third Avenue South. At the conclusion of the banquet, the guests rose and sang the national anthem, "America." (Here again, the decision was to celebrate the years counting from the date of their initial organization in 1880 rather than the date of incorporation in 1882.)

W.B. Mitchell lovingly described the Carnegie building: "This Carnegie building, with its beautiful grounds, its four inner polished granite columns, its handsome mission furniture, the rare art treasures on its walls, the hundreds of volumes on its shelves is a noble monument to the generosity of the Reading Room Society" (W.B. Mitchell, History of Stearns County, 1915).

CHAPTER THREE

Reading Room Civic Concerns Grow Beyond the Library

As time went on, after completion of the Carnegie Library in 1902, the Reading Room Society continued loyal to its commitment to the library, responding to needs of the times. The Society also broadened its scope and increased its other civic work as well. It had earlier included the beautiful park system as one of its chief interests, sponsoring clean-up days in the spring when all the streets, alleys, and vacant lots were cleaned. The Society advocated for systematic collection of garbage and campaigned for meat and milk inspection. This was a nation-wide effort that had been promoted through member organizations of the General Federation of Women's Clubs (GFWC). (The Reading Room Society has had membership in the GFWC since1895. Look to Chapter Five, p. 71 for a more detailed description of its work and relationship with member organizations.)

The New Pure Food and Drug Act was material for a cartoon of the FDA in the early twentieth century. (Cartoon from the Reading Room Society Archives)

As far back as 1901, the Reading Room and Schumann Club members joined in an effort to improve several aspects of the city to beautify and make it more healthful. The first step was to make it clean. The organizations pledged themselves to require businesses and residents to remove from the city limits, collections of ashes, tin cans, and such, for which they might be responsible. They then went to the teachers in public and parochial schools to obtain their cooperation in interesting their pupils in clearing up their yards and adjacent lots and to prevent the scattering of waste papers in the streets. They made the promise that the clubs would provide flowers for the beds in the city parks, providing the city would water and care for them. If the Library Board wished, the clubs would also plant flower beds in the lawn of the library building.

Continuing their campaign, the clubs drew up a petition to present to the City Council, asking that a way be found to collect garbage in the summer months. The garbage problem had become a serious matter, a blemish on the beauty and health of the city; it was important to make some provision in this matter.

There were continuing efforts to convince the city about the need for enforcing city health ordinances. A

Hester Gilman (Mrs. Charles), a Reading Room Society Charter member for whom Hester Park was named. (Photo courtesy Stearns History Museum)

St. Cloud Daily Times article under the headline: "Some Plain Truths," by Mrs. Caroline Bartlette Crane, told the St. Cloud people about the need of reform by local grocers and bakers; the Union School was condemned; the creamery was called bad; and it was stressed that garbage was not properly being handled. (*St. Cloud Daily Times*, circa 1912; article saved in Reading Room Archives, but date not attached.)

Responding to Mrs. Crane's article, a special meeting called by the Reading Room Society turned out a very large crowd at the Opera House. Reading Room president, Mrs. C.L. Atwood, introduced Mrs. Crane, who elaborated on St. Cloud's needed reforms.

In 1914, the health issues of the day were faced. Spitting on the sidewalks was brought to the attention of the city. The long held practice of having one tin cup at public pumps was also questioned as a health risk. "The Reading Room Society says contagion is spread by these violations. Club women will ask officials to enforce the violations" (the *Journal Press*).

Marion S. Jenks, president, in her 1909-1910 annual report to the Society, wrote in summary of the twenty-ninth year: "It has been, we believe, a year of progress. We have been one of the hostess clubs to entertain the State Federation. We have beautified our city parks. We have contributed $300.00 for a scholarship in our Normal School, and $100.00 for the purchase of books by the City Library. We have added $50.00 to an equal amount set apart by the School Board which rendered possible the employment of Mr. Knutson to conduct a boy's class in manual training during the summer months, and we can but feel that the strong interest and pledged support of this society has been one of the determining factors in the decision of the School Board to establish a department of Domestic Science in our Public Schools.

"The Society worked for many changes in the curriculum in the public schools, seeking retention of subjects such as music and fine woodworking when they were going to be removed from the curriculum. In the arts were concert recitals, art exhibits, and lecture courses, under the auspices of the Reading Room. Events were open to the public and took place in the library" (President's, annual report 1908-1909)

In 1910, "Ladies Protest Against School: Ladies Reading Room does not want women's reform school here" (*Journal Press* September 10). The Reading Room protested against locating the proposed women's reform school in close proximity to the men's reformatory, proposing a different location. Instead, they urged the passage of the bill that separated young girls to the State Industrial Home for Girls at Sauk Centre. This met with approval and in August, 1907, Governor Johnson honored the Society by appointing Mrs. George W. Stewart, a Reading Room member, to the Board of Women Visitors for the State Industrial School for Girls. Later, she would be recognized for her long service to the Industrial School for Girls and membership on its board.

Included in its report in 1912, at the thirty-second annual meeting: "The Society during the past year has done an immense

amount of good with anti-tubercular work, assisting visiting nurses. In addition, the Society contributed $100.00 to cover expenses of summer courses in domestic science and manual training. The recently formed Health and Hygiene Committee sold anti-T.B. stamps and Red Cross buttons in January; a tuberculosis exhibit was held in the city in September; the Club secured doctors to present lectures on vital health subjects. They worked to have a medical inspector for the St. Cloud schools and promoted a county sanatorium."

With the business described in the yearly reports, a rigorous program was set up for 1910-1911, an example of how seriously they were taking their goal of growing intellectually:

Program 1910-1911
September 8—Annual Meeting.
September 12—Talk on Caroline Bartlett Crane, Mrs. C.L. Atwood.
October 6—"Shall It Be Opportunity?" Fanny French Morse
October 20—School Census and Health Survey, Mrs. Perry Starkweather

November 3—Maurice Maeterlinck, Characteristics and Influence, "The Blue Bird," Mrs. James Jenks

November 17—Modern Drama in France, Mrs. Martin Molitor

December 1—Edmond Rostand, Exponent of French Thought, "Cyrano de Bergerac," Mrs. Fred Schilplin

December 15—Victorien Sardou, Sketch of his Dramatic Work, "La Tosca," Mrs. S.A. Jones

December 29—Modern Drama in Norway and Sweden. Dr. P.M. Magnuson.

ST. CLOUD READING ROOM HOSTED STATE FEDERATION IN 1919

FOLLOWING WORLD WAR I, in 1919, the State Federation of Women's Clubs met in St. Cloud. The many organizations from towns around the state reported on their club activities. In civic activities, reported by the St. Cloud women, was their work in Baby Welfare. From time to time, they mailed helpful parenting literature to mothers of all registered babies. The committee distributed, through the schools of the city, 24,000 Child Welfare pamphlets. They cooperated with the Council of Defense in conducting the weighing and measuring station for all children under school age, providing exhibits for "Better Babies" at the Benton County Fair, making and supplying baby layettes for the needy of the city.

IN A VERY SPECIAL ACTION, THE SOCIETY ADOPTED A FRENCH CHILD, VICTIM OF WORLD WAR I.

AT THE 1919 ANNUAL MEETING, the following letter translated by Father Thibeault of the St. Cloud Catholic Diocese, from the mother of one of the little French twins adopted by the Society was read:

Lyons-la-for'et, June 16, 1919.

Dear Sir and Friend: I have received your order for 15 francs which you had the kindness to send me, for favor of my young son, Alexander Dedicour. Thank you very much dear benefactor for your generosity toward an unfortunate mother, a stranger to you,. My five children and I will always keep a deep gratefulness for it. This young boy is very proud and happy for what you did in his favor; he repeats often the address of his American benefactor to whom he sends his thanks from the bottom of his heart. Although he is only four years old, he begins to understand the favor that you offered him. I am to buy him at once a pair of shoes to cover his wounded feet. This war caused us to lose everything, and sacrifice all, whilst thinking of our worst horrors, our worst misfortunes, we cannot check our tears.

Tried in our dearest affections, and victims of the war, I have nothing left except five boys—the oldest is 14, the second Ovilon, and third, Leon 8 years, twin boys are 4, Alexander and Joseph, whom I brought to the world in a cellar without any assistance or help, and nursed for three years, without getting one quart of milk.

In spite of the bombardments and brutalities of the Germans, I was able to save their lives in the midst of cruel miseries. It was much useless to give my assistance during the war—and I did not see much of the daylight.

It might interest you dear benefactor, to know that we are from Corevillers, 2 kilometers from Bapume near Arra (Por de Calais). My parents were farmers. It was my good fortune to have my father— just one year ago we were in the midst of the fire, we have been able to save ourselves. Taking anyway the twin children. My father and husband left for Belgium, Germany, and Switzerland—my father succumbed at the French frontier—my husband also died for France on the 24th of May 1916, during the siege of Verdun. My little ones alone have given me the courage to bear to the last—I want to live for them. Although my health is going down—if the hour were coming that I should leave them, I beg of you dear friend to think of them. As to ourselves, your noble name is engraved in our heart. I beg you to believe in our gratitude. My best wishes for health and happiness to yourself and dear family—with my respectful homage.

The dear little Alexander says many good things to his American benefactor and sends his best kisses—Made (Widow) Dedicourt.

On learning the child was one of twins, the Society agreed to take steps to adopt the other child.

INFLUENZA EPIDEMIC IN ST. CLOUD DURING THE WAR.

THE YEAR, 1918-1919 WAS A very active year for the Society. Mrs. A.G. Whitney was elected president. (She declined the second term and Mrs. H.R. Neide was elected president for the year 1919-1920.) Two significant events occurred that kept the Reading Room committees very busy the whole year. In 1918 World War One was winding down, and in November of the same year an influenza epidemic broke out in St. Cloud. In a report to the 1919 annual meeting the following report was given by Mrs. A.A. Wright, secretary:

"During the flu epidemic the St. Cloud Institute, a building owned by and situated across from Immaculate Conception Church, (now, St. Mary's Cathedral), was virtually turned into a hospital. The Institute was staffed with thirty to forty nurses. Benedictine sisters and volunteers, and Reading Room women delivered one hot meal a day to take care of the staff. This required soliciting volunteers to prepare the food, picking up the food from the volunteers, delivering twenty-four dinners a day, to the Institute and returning the pans back to the preparing volunteers. Reading Room did this for fifteen days. Seventy-one people were involved in this effort, with forty from Reading Room Society. Mrs. C.B. Lewis worked right at the Institute until she came

The St. Cloud Institute served as a hospital for influenza victims in 1918-1919. (Photo courtesty Stearns History Museum)

down with the flu at which time Mrs. J.C. Brown took over, but Mrs. Lewis continued to direct the supervision by telephone.

"Reading Room also provided cookies to take to the 'War Camp Committee' in St. Paul and later to the St. Cloud Commercial Club after a local canteen was set up. Over the year, one hundred fifty dozen cookies were delivered. The War Committee was asked for help in preparing Christmas boxes for the service men. The volunteers on this committee spent thirty half-days and seven evenings to complete this task. Reading Room also sponsored three war orphans (two French girls and an Armenian girl) through the War Committee.

"Civic Committee reported that in cooperation with the Commercial Club, Reading Room sponsored Victory gardens by furnishing seed and prizes. St. Cloud Victory Gardens were rated second in the U.S. by the Pure Food Committee: This committee, along with City Health Inspector Paul Scherer, inspected forty to fifty meat markets, grocery stores, bakeries, and creameries once every other month. During the war years, sanitation in food establishments was declining, but with these inspections the cleanliness rating improved considerably.

"We are paying for the support of two French orphans. We have kept up our interest in civic improvement giving our money and support to the community Christmas , money for seeds and prizes for Victory gardens. We are members of the Auto Club and Central Council of Welfare agencies. We have given our annual contribution to the Public Library, this year voting $200.

"We have entertained this spring the Sixth District meeting, paying most of the expense. It was a great success due to the committee's fine work on the social side as well as the regular meetings.

"And we can say with pride that in Reading Room Society it is noticeable—in work done and results achieved." Mrs. A.A. Wright, secretary.

It was also noted in Mrs. Wright's report that as many as eighteen attended each meeting, and there was a long list for membership. Also, the Society purchased $1,750 in Liberty Bonds.

A 1925 Survey Shows Flaws in the
Library System in a Time of Depression

To meet professional standards of the American Library Association, the St. Cloud Library hired a noted librarian from St. Paul to make a study of the St. Cloud Library in 1925. It was pointed out that St. Cloud should have a professionally trained librarian and increased staff. The demands had increased drastically in twenty-five years, and every department of the library "needs to be organized and strengthened," according to the survey report. The methods used were those of an earlier day, and further, "The crying need of the library is the development of an adequate children's department." It also reported that the St. Cloud Library did not meet standards on the number of books available per capita in a city the size of St. Cloud.

Efforts to respond to the survey were met with some difficulty, principally for economic reasons. However, the staff, by 1927, had been increased with a professional librarian, and plans were under way to provide a children's room. With the coming of a full-blown depression also came increased use of the library; circulation in 1931 was an impressive 109,488. Decrease in funds necessitated the end of free library service to non-residents of St. Cloud, which had been the practice since the beginning. There were people who thought that money spent for library purposes was a waste, just a luxury, but they were not successful in their attempts to belittle its value. Librarians, as well as all of the staff, took steep pay cuts during those years.

The increasingly poor economic situation would have held up the opening of the new children's room in the basement of the library if the same group that had so often come to the library's aid in the past had not once again stepped into the breach. In March 1931, "The Librarian reported a gift of $800 from the Reading Room Society, given with the understanding that it was to be used for the purpose of fitting up the children's room which had been indefinitely postponed." The new children's room opened the first of September 1931.

And again, the Reading Room Society, ever faithful supporter of the library, took action on April 24, 1933. According to minutes of the Board: "The Librarian presented a letter from the secretary of the Reading Room Society to the president of the Board, informing the Board that a fund of $4,000 had been set aside by the Society, the interest to be given to the library each year for the purchase of books. A check for sixty dollars($60) was enclosed."

November 5, 1935: Maude Schilplin spoke of "the necessity of creating public opinion which would give thoughtful consideration to the present needs of the library until our commission finds a way to increase the present building . . . we have no branch library to serve our outlying districts as they should be served and encouraged to read." She also spoke of the "importance of the report and of our privilege and responsibility in helping to create public opinion regarding these conditions . . ."

The Depression had created hard times for everyone, including the library staff who in 1933 took a reduction in their salaries. In the next year they took unpaid two-week vacations. By 1935, because of increased use of the library, it was clear that more space was necessary. In addition, growing interest in providing good service to rural areas was an issue to many people. The opportunity to remodel or build an addition to the Library building, became possible when WPA help became available. WPA: Works Progress Administration was a federal program to hire people without work to do jobs that served a community need. It was decided to proceed, using WPA labor with relatively low cost to the city.

ADDITIONAL SPACE IS PROVIDED FOR THE LIBRARY

THE FOLLOWING YEAR, IN 1936, the city acquired the old Unitarian church property located behind the library, with the intention of adding space to the library. However, in 1937, it became clear that the decision to use WPA workers and available government funding was the better plan. So, work began to build an addition to the library building. on the existing property. In 1939 the annex opened, providing considerable additional space for storage of books.

CHAPTER FOUR

A Closer Look at Leaders of the First Fifty Years

$\mathcal{T}$he story of the women of the Reading Room Society has illuminated the history of the "progress" of women in this community; not only in their abilities, but in the acknowledgement of their high hopes and in recognition of their endeavors for the city. The dream and the task of bringing cultural life to this outpost on the Mississippi River, nearly one hundred and fifty years ago, also fell to these women. But, interestingly, when the women won the right to vote, a news item appeared that commended the women on their "good behavior" at the polling place. A remnant of the old attitude continued?

Most of the early women would define themselves as "ladies," a word that suggested breeding, good family, social position, and manners. But the word has become passé. They certainly had all of these qualities. However, it didn't require these attributes when the "ladies" were confronted with the cold blast of Minnesota winters in a roughly made house that didn't protect them from fierce wind and cold. It didn't protect them from the fear of the heat of summer that produced grasshopper invasions and the possibility of Indian uprisings against the people who were taking over their land in the early days of settlement here.

"Woman" connotes a female adult person with all of the human qualities a person might develop. The very early women leaders came during the years of the settlement of St. Cloud. Maria Clarke Waite, for instance, moved to St. Cloud in 1858 when this was a place of hardship, lacking any of the comforts that are taken for granted today. Her story will be the first.

MARIA CLARKE WAITE, READING ROOM SOCIETY'S FIRST PRESIDENT.

MARIA WAS BORN IN HUBBARDSTON, Massachusetts, July 13, 1834, daughter of Dr. and Mrs. Sheppard Clarke, and lived there until she married Mr. Joseph Paige. They moved to Barre, Massachusetts, where they lived for a year before they turned westward and located in Jerseyville, Illinois. Her mother, Mary Ann Dickinson Clarke, had relocated in the west earlier, moving to Jerseyville where she was widowed.

Maria and her mother were among the great movement westward before the railroad had reached the West, with only the rigors of travel by wagon and horses or oxen, or by boat down the Ohio River to East St. Louis. Mr. Paige died in 1858, so Maria's stay in Jerseyville was short. With her mother, the two women moved to St. Cloud where they had relatives. It is hard to imagine the hardships of the trip from New York, then the loss of her husband and the move upriver from Illinois for the young widow and her also recently widowed mother. But many more hardships would follow.

About two years later, in 1860, Maria married Henry Chester Waite. Waite's autobiography described the vicious Minnesota winter and his plans to go back to New York where he had grown up, but a lovely spring and summer influenced him to stay. Two sons were born to them, Chester and Clarke. Son, Chester died young, but Clarke grew up and lived at the family farm just outside of town. The year after Maria became Mrs. Waite, the Indian Outbreak occurred and the Civil War had started. President Lincoln was calling for volunteers which made the choice between patriotism and self-defense very difficult. Waite decided to remain and protect his young family from Indian attacks. The defenders had no attack on their homes, but he and other settlers marched into the countryside and gave some relief to settlers who were attacked.

Maria Clarke Waite, first president of the Society, circa 1890. (Photo courtesy Stearns History Museum)

Her marriage must have been filled with hard work and turmoil of the times, but she raised her children in that environment at the side of a man who engaged in many occupations—from farming and milling to law and local politics to becoming a state legislator. Waite was away for long stretches of time; eventually, he put aside his law practice for still other pursuits.

In his autobiography, he describes a love affair during his college years with a woman whom he continued to love all his life and lost because he was too busy to follow through with marriage. When he did go back, she had married another. That, he admitted, was a sadness that he carried with him into his marriage to Maria and throughout his life.

Maria Waite was a woman of exceptional ability. Her tastes were along intellectual lines as were those of her husband which made a compatible marriage possible. She had been educated in Hubbardston and at the Academy at Petersham, and it was noted in her biography that she was fond of good literature.

In 1880 she was at the meeting at Mrs. Helen Moore's house when forty-four members of the Library Association met to form the St. Cloud Reading Room Society. "She was elected the first president, (of the Society) which she has been instrumental in organizing and in giving the solid foundation that has made it so much of a force for good in this community." (Old Settlers' Association 1909 at the time of her death.) She was one of the few wives of early pioneers who enrolled their names as members of the Pioneer Association which kept records of enrollees' biographies and their deaths.

Henry Chester Waite the first lawyer in St. Cloud. As time went on, he was active in many businesses, political ventures and was a very prominent citizen of the city. He is quoted in William Mitchell's *History of Stearns County* having written about social conditions which prevailed during the first winter of St. Cloud's history—the winter of 1855-1856—in which he said: "The winter passed away and there was much merriment among the people. Nearly all were strangers to each other—all were poor beginners in life's struggle—social equality existed everywhere. There were no attempts to ostracize this one on account of nationality, dress, or lack of education. The barriers of so-called civilization were obliterated; at least they were wholly absent during that first winter's sojourn in St. Cloud. We had our social gatherings, games, dancing, etc., but there was no card playing as an amusement. It was a democracy of individuals and ideas brought together from all parts of the country" (*History of Stearns County*, William Mitchell, p. 1443).

H.C. Waite, St. Cloud's first lawyer. (Photo courtesy Stearns History Museum)

Mᴀɴʏ ᴏf ᴛʜᴇ ᴡᴏᴍᴇɴ ᴡʜᴏ were very active in Reading Room and many other community organizations, were educated and had become professional in work that was open to them—chiefly nursing and teaching. However, nearly always their biographies mention retirement from their working careers before they married and had families. It is mentioned as the normal process, which of course it was. And, on marrying, the women took their husbands' names as their own, which was a longtime practice. Mrs. W.B. Mitchell, was never Emily Mitchell, except with close women friends. A list of all the members of Reading Room from the very beginning would be a long list of men's names. The annual yearbooks listed members by husband's names, but in the 1970s these were followed by the women's given names. Finally, it became practice to give the women's names first, followed by the husbands'.

The Reading Room has always been an organization that skillfully conducted its business. The members were well read, had programs that were enlightening, regarding local, national and world issues. They made their decisions as to the work they did in the community, how they invested their money. Not to be forgotten, at their organizing in 1880, was one of their guiding principles: their desire to be a strong social component of their Society.

Many of the husbands, of course, were leaders in business, in professions and in community organizations. The women brought the influence of their husbands' reputations, which must have been very helpful, as they presented their plans to town council meetings. Of the first forty-six women who were introduced in Chapter One of this book, at the birth of the Reading Room Society, most had husbands who, by 1882, had proven leadership in their fields . Six of the charter members were unmarried.

Mrs. Emily Whittlesey Mitchell, Elected Vice President at That First Meeting

Emily Whittlesey, was born to the very prominent Ohio family of William A. Whittlesey and Jane (Husted) Whittlesey . She married William B. Mitchell in Marietta, Ohio, on December 7, 1871.

William and Emily moved to St. Cloud, Minnesota, where William had purchased a home before their marriage. This was where they raised their ten children. (Two died before reaching maturity.) It was a large house across First Avenue from the elder Mitchells. A daughter, Ruth, converted her grandparents' home into "Grandma's Garden" where people enjoyed "tea (or box lunch) under the oak trees, asters and dahlias." This continued from 1922 to 1934. William Mitchell's home and his parents' home were razed in 1957 to make room for Mitchell Hall, at St. Cloud State University.

Emily served two terms as president of the Reading Room: 1898 to 1899 and 1899 to 1900.

Mrs. Alice Eastman, President of Reading Room at the Building of the Carnegie Library

Mrs. Alice May (Alvah) Eastman, as president, provided leadership when the Reading Room negotiated for a Carnegie Grant. Alice May was born in Anoka County, Minnesota, the oldest of seven children. Her parents, with the older members of the family, were pioneers from Maine. As a young girl of sixteen, she taught in a country school, and

Emily Whittlesley with her bridesmaids, Laura Jallaher, Mrs. Hale, and Mary Edgerton, at the time of her marriage to William Bell Mitchell in 1871 in Marietta, Ohio, where she had grown up. (Photo courtesy Stearns History Museum)

she helped to support her family and to educate her younger siblings. Later, she was a member of St. Cloud Normal School faculty. Alice married Mr. Alvah Eastman on September 5, 1892, and retired from teaching. The Eastmans had three children, a son and two daughters.

Alice was a very prominent woman socially, and in service to her community and church . She was a member of Unity Church, and

Sunshine Society for the needy. Prominent in the Reading Room Society, she was a member since 1894, and in 1901 she served as president of the Society and played a part in securing the land purchase that made it possible to build the Carnegie Library. She provided leadership for the founding of the library and for the part the Reading Room would continue to play in its future. She was a member of Sorosis, St. Cloud Pioneer Study Club, Daughters of the American Revolution, was librarian for several years and member of the Minnesota Federation of Women's Clubs. She died at her home at 711 Fifth Avenue South February 2, 1935.

The following tribute to Mrs. Eastman was written by Fred Schilplin, publisher of the *St. Cloud Times*: "There has come to the happy Times-Journal family a great sorrow. Mrs. Eastman, beloved wife of Alvah Eastman, died Saturday afternoon. Peacefully rest came to a devoted wife and mother. If there ever was a woman who glorified the name of 'Mother' it was Mrs. Eastman. All that the sweet word of 'Mother' means to mankind in sacrifice and love was embodied in her soul. Words are futile to express what should be said in tribute to her as a mother . . .

The Mitchell family home in the Barden Park Neighborhood in south St. Cloud. (1885 Photo courtesy Stearns History Museum)

"For her life's partner she created for more than fifty years an ideal American home. That home she made radiant with her tender mother love. Into that home came happy children. All their lives she ministered to them. Fate was unkind, and these loved ones to whom she had given so much of her strength and mother love preceded her in death. Thus all her life was a life of a mother's sacrifice and in the making of that sacrifice it was given to her to find her own happiness, her own peace and contentment. There can be no greater mother love than this. Her life's work is ended, but her memory will long endure by all who know the story of that life . . .

> "Long, long be my heart with such memories fil'ld!
> Like the vase in which roses have once been distill'd—
> You may break, you may shatter the vase if you will,
> But the scent of the roses will hang round it still."

MEMORIAL APPEARED IN THE *RED WING DAILY REPUBLICAN*
MRS. EASTMAN PASSES TO REST

"MINNESOTA'S NEWSPAPER FRATERNITY learns with sorrow that Mrs. Alvah Eastman, wife of the editor of the *St. Cloud Times* and *Journal Press* has passed to the beyond. The Eastman family are among the oldest and best known newspaper people of the Northwest and are respected most highly and loved by all who have met them at Journalistic gatherings and otherwise during the past half century.

"Mrs. Eastman always was her husband's pal and no doubt was responsible for a large measure of the success which her husband has achieved as a writer and editor. Possessed of highest ideals, her sympathetic influence has been reflected in Mr. Eastman's exceedingly impressive work for his community and his State. . . . The memory of that noble woman, who has passed away after such a long life of consecration to her cherished ideals of helpfulness and sisterhood, with the devotion to husband and his responsibilities, will remain as a beacon light for him and for others to look back to with memories that will comfort and which will endure."

Alice's husband, Alvah Eastman, was born in Lowell Center, Maine, in 1858. He came to Anoka, Minnesota, in 1880 to work for the newspaper there owned by an uncle. It was in Anoka that he met his future wife, Alice May. He became a state representative in 1889 and moved to St. Cloud in 1892 where he purchased the *St. Cloud Daily Journal Press*, one of the state's most influential newspapers, from William Bell Mitchell. Eastman was known for his sensible, well-written editorials. He was the receiver of the U.S. Land Office in St. Cloud for ten years, president of the St. Cloud Park Board as well. He helped organize the Boy Scouts and American Red Cross chapters, also established scholarships at the high school and St. Cloud Teachers College.He gave land and money to the college for Selke Field, Talahi Lodge, and additional recreational grounds, and he also gave land for a men's dormitory. Eastman Hall, a physical education building on the campus, and Eastman Park near Lake George were named in his honor.

As time went on, a strong affinity grew between the women of the Normal School and the Reading Room Society and their husbands. And, the Normal School grew, from St. Cloud Normal School, to the Teachers' College, and finally, to St. Cloud State University.

George Selke was president of the college, but the field was named for his wife, Carol, who was president of the Reading Room Society in 1934-1935. George died December 24, 1939.

ALICE WHITLOCK WHITNEY (MRS. A.G.) WAS A PROMINENT "GRAND LADY" OF ST. CLOUD

ALICE WHITLOCK WHITNEY WOULD probably rebel at being cast as "Grand Lady," but she went ahead of everybody else in the work she accomplished during her many active years in St. Cloud, and always in great style. She was born in Leicester, New York, in 1868 and grew up there .

When time came for Alice to obtain further education, she came to St. Cloud because an aunt, her mother's sister, was teaching at the Normal School. She could live with her sister and brother-in-law, Mrs. and Mrs. Frank Tolman, who had a home in the Barden Park neighborhood near the river. It was at the Normal School that she met Albert Whitney, fell in love and brought him back to New York for a Christmas-time wedding in 1891. They too settled in the Barden Park neighborhood. This was also near many other St. Cloud Reading Room members. They built an exquisite "modern" colonial house where they brought up three children and later entertained the next generation.

She became a consummate hostess, offering hospitality, not only to friends in the many organizations in which she became involved but also to prominent out-of-town guests whom she introduced to the St. Cloud community. Among those who stayed at the Whitney house, were Eleanor Roosevelt, wife of President Franklin D., famous singer Marion Anderson, and other musicians and public figures who visited the city, at a time when a black person would not be allowed to stay at a hotel.

Alice was an early member of Reading Room Society, having joined in 1898 and serving as president in 1918-1919. She was also a member of Sorosis, Daughters of the American Revolution, Minnesota Historical Society, Children's Home Society of St. Paul as a board

Whitney Home. (Photo courtesy Stearns History Museum)

member, Stearns County Historical Society, and was an active worker in the Camp Fire Girls. She was also an active member of First Presbyterian Church.

Albert G. Whitney (A.G.) was a very successful entrepreneur, in the tradition of the "Self-Made Man." "The Amazing thing," according to Sister Owen Lundblad, *Times* columnist, "is that nothing came through inheritance." He began his career in real estate, loans, and insurance. In 1900 he purchased the St. Cloud Power and Heating plant on Fifth Avenue North to distribute electricity to St. Cloud and Sauk Rapids. Then, the Gas and Electric Company, and in 1908 he pur-

Alice Wheelock Whitney at the airport dedication. (Photo courtesy Stearns History Museum)

Top: Eleanor Roosevelt visit to *St. Cloud. Times* editor Fred Schilplin accompanied her to the Great Northern Depot from the Whitney Home. Bottom: Marian Anderson, noted contralto, also a guest of the Whitneys, William S. Weber, Miss Myrl Carlsen.

chased the St. Cloud Power Company and the dam as well. All of these became the Public Service Company, forerunner of Northern States Power Company.

He and Alice raised their family in the handsome brick "modern" colonial residence which they had built on First Avenue adjacent to the St. Cloud State University campus. It was subsequently turned over to St. Cloud State University for student housing and later, office space. After Albert's death, Alice took charge of another generous gift to the city. It had been something she and Albert had planned before his death: land on the north side to be used for an airfield was given in 1929. The airfield was outgrown as the city grew. In 1967 a modern new airport was built east of the city. The original land donated for airport became parkland again. The many places named for "Whitney" throughout the city remind citizens of St. Cloud of the generous people who bore the name.

Albert Whitney died at age sixty-one in 1922. Alice lived to be eighty-six and died in 1954. They both served out their lives in St. Cloud. Three of their grandchildren continue to have an interest in the family and their St. Cloud background:

Pauline (Mrs. Cargill MacMillan) of Wayzata, Lois (Mrs. Allan B. Forbes) of Cambridge, Massachusetts, and son, Wheelock of Wayzata. The family donated and furnished a room at the Stearns County History Museum and Resource Center to display their mother's life in St. Cloud and the many activities of the family.

"Ladies" were "Ladylike"

THE WOMEN OF THE READING ROOM SOCIETY might appear to the reader as rather humorless as they purposefully pursued their goals. They were practical, efficient and, try as one might, very few laughable situations will be discovered. Their meetings were planned and printed for the coming year with the full program of speakers announced in advance. Don't forget—a lady must not laugh or talk too much. Ladies' manners prevailed; correct dress and behavior were defined. Society members could never laugh at them for these habits. Many of the older Reading Room women in current membership grew up in an era that closely followed on those that are described—at least their mothers did—and they set that example. Not one of them would go anyplace hatless, gloveless, or wearing trousers! The 1970s changed these styles with the coming of the "Hip Generation."

Women who continue to be active in the Society beyond the age of seventy or eighty, when interviewed, are quick to recall those times when such order prevailed—and have expressed their wish that they could return to some traditional behavior. But the newer members are happily relaxed in the new culture. Time will tell if this brings the same surges of creative enterprise—and humor—into the organization. Carrying that thought a little further, there must have been some laughs along the line when they outsmarted the City Council on various occasions. But a lady wouldn't let them know. The careful decorum of a meeting in the "old days" dictated (non-verbally) that nobody spoke without standing and waiting to be acknowledged by the president; and all politely remained seated until the president arose from the table after dinner. The latter practice does continue on in the twenty-first century, although others are on the wane or have been dismissed.

Women of Reading Room today in the twenty-first century look for a list of these gracious old practices, buried somewhere, perhaps in the archives. But the archives contains no such list. Of course, there were things women learned from their mothers as expected behavior. This, remember, is the history of women whose story began nearly one hundred fifty years ago, with the settlement of St. Cloud This was accomplished by people from the East who started out in log houses, but who were soon building houses that could accommodate thirty-five to forty-five people for a meeting, dinner, and an evening of conversation and musical entertainment. And they met twice a month until the 1970s!

The women began with the desire to recover the life they knew in the long-established communities from which they had come. And they did just that. They had the churches they knew "back home." By

the early years of the twentieth century, names of members of the Irish
Catholic community were appearing on member lists. The German
names began to appear soon after that. It is difficult to catch a glimpse
into their lives, except to know that many of the women in positions
of leadership had husbands who were successful; their style of life was
reflected in many of their elegant homes that remain on the Southside.

MEMORIES OF OLDER READING ROOM MEMBERS ARE PRESERVED.

IN THE YEAR, 2007, DR. BARBARA SAIGO, then president of St. Cloud
Reading Room, assigned a project to three older members who were
members during a time of transition. They were asked to meet together
and respond to a set of subjects she gave them to obtain a clear picture
of the mid-twentieth century Reading Room Society. Following are
the notes taken by Mrs. Beulah Rose Hutchens (1970) in conversation
with Mrs. Gloria Laughlin (1954) and Mrs. Ann Didier (1974). In the
1970s many of the "old traditions" were continuing, when these
women were in their early years of belonging, others were being questioned. Some items are included from other interviews as noted. Others, those in capital letters, are those that Dr .Saigo recommended for
discussion.

MEMBERSHIP RESPONSIBILITIES AND EXPECTA-
TIONS: "Every member should serve on a committee and take responsibility of giving a report. Since our membership is larger, the committees
will be larger, but then you won't be called on to report as often.

"We met twice a month. Members held membership for life.
That had to be changed because even if a member could not be active,
she could not be replaced until she died. Some years it was very hard
to invite new members, even with a long list of people waiting.

("Reading Room was a more closely knit group of women,
leaders in St. Cloud. The formality of the organization made it different
from others and made it 'fun' to belong to. The activities of the organization impacted people in the entire community." Beulah Rose
Hutchens's Interview with Erica Ashman and Constance Crane.)

SAMPLE MEETING AGENDA: "Just follow the parliamentary procedure; the secretary and treasurer should give monthly reports as they do, followed by a brief business meting and then have committee reports at each meeting. When I first became a member, we didn't have as many committees but each committee gave a report at the meeting. We learned so much from the reports it was like having another program. Norma Luckemeyer, with her artistic talent, usually had an interesting visual to enhance her reports, regardless of the committee she was on.

PROTOCOL FOR INTRODUCTION OF PROGRAM AND THANKING SPEAKERS: "The member who invited the speaker introduced the person and expressed thanks and presented the gift, usually monetary. The program committee planned the programs around the committees so that each program was an enhancement of the committee. The Civic Committee usually asked someone involved with city or community activities. Education, someone from the school system, kindergarten through college, providing a wide variety. Library was always an interesting program since that was the basis of Reading Room endeavors. The program committee also chose a theme for the year for the speakers: e.g., in 2009, for instance, the speakers were chosen to relate to the theme suggested by GFWC, regarding the domestic violence awareness in this country. (As an example, Judge Charles Flin described the work of family court on the response to this subject in the Stearns County Court.)"

PROTOCOL FOR MEALS AND MEETINGS: "When you wanted to speak, you stood and addressed the chair, waited for recognition,

Beulah Rose Hutchens in conversation about times past with Gloria Laughlin and Anne Didier in 2009. (Photo by Pat Witte)

then spoke. There was no undercurrent of conversation during the meeting. Before the meeting and during dinner there was much visiting. One of the oldest customs that we still observe and is unique to Reading Room: after dinner, the president stands as a sign of 'being excused from the table' so to speak. If someone found it necessary to leave beforehand, she spoke with the president before the meeting. We are glad it is still observed and hope it will always be a part of Reading Room.

"Another custom, no longer observed, was that each member called the hostess two days before the meeting if she was unable to attend; if you didn't call, it meant that you would be there. Wine or liquor was never served at Reading Room. I believe it was a silent, mutual agreement that for those few hours per year, abstinence was not a hardship.

"When the organization first began, they met in the homes twice a month with the hostess serving dinner. Some of the husbands were invited to dine with them. They met year around when I became a member in 1970. However, not everyone had a house large enough to accommodate the group so the hostess had the meeting at the Germain Hotel or the Moore Hostess House near the college. Those who could, continued to serve in their homes."

"In the sixties and seventies, in response to the space problem, the Vocational-Technical High school was a part of the St. Cloud School District. It was discovered that the department of food preparation and service would be willing to serve dinners for Reading Room meetings that could be held there at the school. It was a good practical experience for future chefs and waiters to use their skills. The women loved the setup, and it was repeated for a few years. Then, the Teachers College invited the Society to use its dining room as well. However, when the owners of local restaurants objected to the loss of business, meeting at local restaurants and clubs became standard practice." (Notes from a discussion with Beaulah Rose Hutchens in October 2009 pkw.)

"Eventually, as life styles changed, some of the members went away for the summer so the Society did not meet in the summer months. Then it moved to a once-a-month schedule, and as times continued to change, two hostesses took responsibility each month for reservations and planning. However, members continued to call the hostess if unable to attend. Now, of course, the hostess calls each member, who pays for her own meal.

OTHER CUSTOMS AND TRADITIONS: "Membership in Reading Room was a special privilege For many years membership was limited to fifty members for entertainment and program space. Membership has always been by invitation. When people were less mobile, there were few changes in membership. When a name was proposed they have always used the cards to propose a name, but if there was not an opening, the card was put in an envelope with a date and the name of the member proposing it, so they could be voted on in order. Before the vote was taken, the proposing member stood and told about the person she would like to invite. Even if you didn't know her, you knew the five ladies who had vouched for her. It was often said that you proposed with knowledge and voted with faith. When the vote was taken, the secretary sent an invitation, and two people were asked to visit the candidate to tell her about Reading Room. She then wrote her letter of acceptance and someone brought her to the meeting. The process took at least two months. A member must belong to the Society for a year before being eligible to propose a name, and then a wait of twelve months must pass before proposing another name. This is still contained in the bylaws. I don't ever remember anyone being rejected.

"At the death of a member, a memorial tribute is written for her, read at a meeting then placed in the History book. A memorial book is purchased and placed in the library in her memory with a special book plate. Her place in membership is vacant for three months.

"Since Reading Room is basically a study group, we did not have Christmas parties; we had a regular meeting and assumed that everyone belonged to other groups for parties.

"The first bus trip to Chanhassen was just for members and was well attended. It was not an annual event. Another time we at-

tended the Old Log Theater in Excelsior. The Chanhassen trip for a play at the Chanhassen Dinner Theater is now an annual event and quite often we have as many guests as members.

"I've always been grateful to the five members who gave me the gift of membership. I have always appreciated the graciousness and wisdom of the members. I have gained much by my membership in Reading Room and hope you have. I hope that we can continue to grow in wisdom and charity."

Signed by Beulah Rose Hutchens (1970), who wrote the transcript of the meeting. (February 2007 Ann Didier [1974] Gloria Laughlin [1954])

"I'M MORE INTENSE ON ISSUES THAN OTHERS . . ." Gloria Boch Laughlin.

Gloria was born in April of 1913 in Faribault, Minnesota, and at age ninety-five, she easily recounted her life to the Reading Room members, Constance Crane and Helen Catton. The following are notes from their taped recording of their conversation.

Gloria's father, John Bock, a banker, was educated in Switzerland; her mother was a teacher. Gloria graduated from Faribault High School with honors and special interests in speech, history, and journalism. She went on to the University of Minnesota and majored in Journalism and History.

While visiting friends in St. Cloud when she was a young woman, she was told about the Reading Room Society and the outstanding women in the organization. When she moved here with her husband and family in 1940, she was sponsored by her friend and invited to join the Society. The Reading Room recognized talent when they met her, and she was elected president within her first five years of membership.

Until the mid-fifties, Gloria recalled the club continued meeting in the homes of members twice a month. Two members were responsible for planning and serving the supper. It was sometimes catered by

(opposite) A book plate inserted in books donated to the library in memory of deceasd members, a practice continued to this day. (Courtesy the Reading Room Society Archives)

local women. It became very crowded in some of the homes with a great deal of moving of chairs around to accommodate the crowd. Some of the taboos that continued at that time was the use of first names. The women were "Mrs. Laughlin," "Mrs. Bastien," and so forth. But when Mrs. Bastien became president in 1966, she changed that. She established the use of first names. The membership list continued with husband's name, however, followed by first names of the women.

Gloria noted that the seventy-fifth anniversary of the Reading Room Society in 1957 took place at the St. Cloud Reformatory. The director lived in a house on the property, and it was a lovely affair. It was written up in the *St. Cloud Times*. The newspaper columnist made

Gloria Laughlin, president from 1964 to 1966. (Photo by Pat Witte)

a bi-weekly report of the Reading Room meetings in her Friday column, sometimes giving detailed accounts of the committee reports and speakers as well as social items.

The most important project then, from the fifties until 1979, was working on the bond issue to build a new library. It had failed five times when it finally passed and the new library was built on Fourth Avenue and St. Germain Street in St. Cloud.

Gloria was usually active on the International Relations Committee over the years, although not solely. She was always hopeful that the reports on the nation and world had an impact on the members, that they broadened the scope of their interests. It is different today as the degree of involvement on social issues has lessened. There is less reporting on social issues. "I'm more intense on issues than others," said Gloria.

This was a time when women were starting to be accepted in traditionally men's positions, and Gloria found her place in that movement. She was the first woman to work as a district representative for the Republican Party. She was the second woman to serve on the vestry of the Episcopalian Church. She hoped she served as a model for other women to step up into what had always been the province of men.

The most valuable gift of her years of membership in the Reading Room was the diversity among the women and good friendships and inspiration from many people, a veritable "continuing education." She was also grateful for marvelous, dedicated enthusiasm of leadership in her active years.

She knows that some members have negative attitudes toward membership in GFWC, critical of paying dues to the Federation. However, Gloria believes that the national organization has done a lot of good, particularly with small community groups by providing program ideas and leadership. She saw changes in Reading Room that she attributed to the programs of the General Federation of Women's Clubs.

She is grateful for having taken part in the move from the Carnegie to the New Library. It was inspiring to come to know the background of the Society and its history of the women who had the foresight to work so hard over the years for a "book-starved community." (From an interview with Gloria Laughlin in 2008 by M. Constance Crane and Helen Catton.)

"MY MOST IMPORTANT REASON FOR JOINING WAS TO WORK FOR SUPPORT FOR A NEW LIBRARY." Beulah Rose Hutchens.

Beulah Rose Hutchens was born in September of 1925 on a Kentucky farm, where she grew up with her parents and two brothers. Beulah Rose received her education at Iowa State Teachers College where she prepared herself to teach kindergarten. Her husband was also a teacher, at Sauk City High School, Kentucky. In St. Cloud she taught kindergarten part time, and her husband taught business courses at the Vocational Technical District 742 School. At that time the rule was that a husband and wife could not both teach in the same school district full time.

Beulah Rose has been a member of Reading Room since 1970. Ethel Grogan, a longtime member, placed her name for membership when she was forty-five years old and of course, she was received in the Society. When Beulah Rose joined the Reading Room Society in 1970, her first assignment was as publicity chair. She made an appointment with Mr. Frederick C. Schilplin, who was about to retire. He introduced her to the new editor of the *Times*, Harold Scholkopf, with whom she would be working. After the many years of having a "Society Page" editor who covered in detail the activities and meetings of the Reading Room, she was surprised to be told that the new editor was not interested in writing about "old lady organizations." She was not fifty at the time, stunned and angry at his diatribe. She was unaware that, at that point in

Vote yes! Display in the window of Fandel's Department Store, circa 1965. (Photo courtesy Stearns History Museum)

Beulah Rose Hutchens mentors new member, Karel Helgeson, 2010. (Photo by Pat Witte)

history, this was occurring in newspapers across the country, a result of shortage of newsprint, higher costs, a greater feeling for allowing more voices to be heard rather than the perceived entitlement of women's societies to receive more space than they deserved, compared with other news of the day.

In addition, when Beulah Rose joined the Society the Carnegie Library was about to be torn down. She came at a pivotal time in the history of the Reading Room and the Library System. The principle effort was to achieve voter approval to make it possible to build a new, up-to-date and larger library. People had loved the Carnegie Library, almost to a fault—and now to demolish it? This effort was her main reason for joining the Society, in order to join the effort to bring out the vote that engaged its members. She was a member of AAUW, an organization also prominent in the fight for a larger, modern new building. Mrs. Doris Otto, a past president of Reading Room and members of both organizations, joined her in the effort. They found many others, men and women, who became members of a new organization, Friends of the Library. Sixty-five Friends of the Library members were organized for the sole purpose of bringing out the vote for the next bond issue by emphasizing the community need for a larger, more up-to-date library. Thus, after some failed attempts over several years, and with additional numbers of people out speaking to organizations throughout the city, this effort finally was successful.

After the library was built on St. Germain and Fourth Avenue, the Friends organization became a volunteer arm of the library. Members were given specific work to do such as replacing books on shelves and other tasks in the library. In the following years, the group has grown, adding many helpful jobs.

Beulah Rose feels that, over the years, the Reading Room has been a more closely knit group of women and leaders in St. Cloud. The activities of the organization "impacted" people in the whole community. During her years, she has served in nearly every position of leadership in the organization.

She said her family was always interested in what she did. They called her a "professional volunteer." One can understand why when she names the long list of offices she has held in the city as well as Reading Room. Among the city offices, she was on the City Planning Commission for thirteen years, County Commissioner, the Park and Recreation Board, and the Library Board. In all of these she held the office of chair. A health condition finally put a stop to that level of commitment, but that didn't stop Beulah Rose. She and her husband both felt that it was important to give back to the community in which they raised their family. She reduced her endeavors to less time-consuming projects and avoided taking the stressful positions.

Beulah Rose said the greatest gift of the Reading Room to her has been the "gift of friendship.

CHAPTER FIVE

The Reading Room Society Celebrated Its Golden Jubilee in Style in 1932.

ary Elizabeth Crandall Atwood (Mrs. Clarence), toastmistress at the Golden Jubilee celebration at the Breen Hotel, spoke to the spirit of veneration for age that prevails in the Reading Room Society. It was a night of tribute to the pioneer members of the society and those women who worked with it in the same spirit as the founders for fifty years.

Among the honored guests were two charter members who were still active: Mrs. D.H. Freeman and Miss Isabel Lawrence. Mrs. H.C. Ervin, who joined in 1889, a forty-one-year member was present. Mrs. Atwood, 1891, thirty-nine years a member, was president and also State Federation president. Mrs. C.B. Lewis chaired this celebration with a committee of fourteen women. At the affair, Mrs. Atwood introduced Mrs. H.C. Bowing, who read *Highlights of Our History* by Maude Schilplin (Mrs. Fred). Historian of the Reading Room Society (whose absence was necessitated by a death in her family), Mrs. Schilplin wrote: "Madame Chairman, Members of the Reading Room Society, Past Presidents and Honored Guests: It is with added pleasure that we are privileged on this memorable occasion, our fiftieth anniversary, to greet our husbands. All honor to the club husbands." She sited two previous great social occasions in Reading Room history: At twenty-one years when

Mary Elizabeth Crandall (Mrs. Clarence) Atwood was Toastmistress for the Golden Anniversary Gala at the Breen Hotel. (Photo courtesy *St. Cloud Times*)

"We, as Colonial dames, with powdered hair and long flowing trains, entertained our husbands at an elaborate Progressive Tea at Unity

Church. It was an Andrew Carnegie affair when stories of past achievements and dreams of future conquests were delightfully mingled in the evening's program." It was the celebration of the anticipation of the $25,000 Carnegie Library, which was about to be built. Mrs. Alvah Eastman, president at that time, also welcomed the guests to the celebration in 1901.

"The second great social highlight was a musicale and banquet that marked our thirtieth anniversary. The affair was held at the spacious home of Mrs. A.L. Riley on Third Avenue. Our husbands were honored guests then as well. The active charter members present were: Mesdms. W.B. Mitchell, C.A. Gilman, N.P. Clarke, John Coates, D.H Freeman, Miss Martha Whitman, and Miss Isabel Lawrence."

Mrs. Bowing continued from the words of Mrs. Schilplin's "Historical Outline": "This Golden Anniversary is the third social highlight."

Maude Schilplin, historian for the Reading Room Society and former president. (Photo courtesy of Yvonne Schilplin)

Mrs. Schilplin honored the special guests who were the husbands who had generously supported, guided and encouraged the women's work. "It has been said," she continued, "by some critics (not by our husbands, of course) that women don't know the value of a dollar; they are poor financiers; they cannot stick to a project long enough to carry it through to a successful finish." Mrs. Schilplin's "Highlights" outlined the history of the Library Association that started in 1865 in which the Reading Room had its origin, and the Reading Room Society that was organized in 1880 and was then celebrating the fiftieth anniversary of its incorporation. She paid tribute to the ladies who were loyal members throughout its history and brought to fruition the first St. Cloud Public Library in 1901, the Carnegie Library, dear to the memory of St. Cloud citizens. The many members who had gone on to take leadership positions in the city, county, and state were remembered. Following is a partial list of women who, in 1932, had shown leadership in the community, women who had also taken roles of responsibility in the Reading Room Society:

Mrs. Mary Stewart, one of the honored guests, a former president of Reading Room, was the superintendent of the State Industrial Home for Girls at Sauk Centre.

Mrs. C.L. Atwood was honored by Minnesota club women when she was chosen as state president in 1913. She had been chairman of various clubs and was then president of the League of Women Voters.

Miss Marianne Clarke, the only member whose mother was a charter member had been appointed state chairman of the Poetry division of Minnesota Federated Clubs.

Mrs. C.C. Dragoo was the first woman in St. Cloud to be president of the City Council and was then the only woman council person. She was also the leader of Washington P.T.A. for several years, and then president of the general council of P.T.A.

Mrs. A.N. Farmer a former secretary of the Society had been writing for several years for prominent school publications.

Mrs. Al Tschumperlin, a former president, was organizing president of the St. Cloud College Club and the Woman's Guild. She was then assistant city librarian.

Mrs. Colie Guy was at the head of the largest P.T.A., of Technical High School.

Mrs. Leonard Williams was president of the Twentieth Century Club, the largest civic organization in the city.

Mrs. George Cashman was president of the Cathedral P.T.A. and vice-president of the state P.T.A.

Mrs. William Sartell, another former president, was at the head of the Sartell Civic League and a leader in her community.

Mrs. C.S. Olds, prominent officer in many church organizations, headed the Sunshine Society.

Miss Estelle Pattison was secretary of the Board of Charities and at the head of the Morris Home, a city institution.

Mrs. H.C. Bowing, president, headed the work of Conservation in Stearns County.

Mrs. E. Everett Clark, president, was former Sixth District president of Federated Clubs and had been leader in several Red Cross campaigns there.

BEWARE! MISS ISABEL LAWRENCE recalled coming to St. Cloud from New York City in September 1879. "I found myself a member of a delightful group of Normal teachers recently arrived from cities of New England and the Middle West. We had been warned by the Grundies of the East to beware of the wild and wooly West, that we would find (wild) Indians in St. Cloud and hear the squeaking Red River wagons in relays going north. As for climate, boiling water thrown up in winter, came down in icicles and your breath froze on your pillow at night. To our disgust we never saw an Indian nor heard a Red River cart. We had no difficulty in keeping warm, and fell in love with St. Cloud at first sight." Miss Lawrence was a Charter Member of the Reading Room Society.

Isabel Lawrence became director of the Normal School in 1879, shortly after she came to St. Cloud. Lawrence Hall, built in 1884, was named for her. In 1913 she became director of the Riverside

Isabel Lawrence, a teacher for whom the St. Cloud State University building was named. She was a charter member of the Reading Room in 1880. (Photo courtesy Stearns History Museum)

Lawrence Hall at St. Cloud State University. (Photo courtesy Stearns History Museum)

Model school, the new school for training teachers. The "wild and wooly West" did not daunt this lady.

GENERAL FEDERATION OF WOMEN'S CLUBS

Mrs. Schilplin's "Historical Outline" further noted: "It is from the ranks of the pioneer Federated clubs, like the Reading Room Society, that our women have been trained for leadership and cooperation."

Looking over the activities and the women involved at the celebration of the first fifty years of the St. Cloud Reading Room, a Federation member since 1895, one can understand in Mrs. Schilplin's reference to the "training for leadership and cooperation," that Federated clubs, like the Reading Room, have done just that. In the early years, problems of the time, such as the need for inspection of meat, and other laws affecting health issues, were addressed through the General Federation of Women's Clubs system, which urged local groups to act on them in their communities. GFWC set the tone, and the example as well as providing training for the clubs throughout the country when towns were growing and new problems arose that needed attention. Also, through the Federation, nationwide efforts for so many initiatives were acted upon through state or local organizations. This was particularly helpful in the early years of the twentieth century when women were new to taking a public stand on public issues.

Then, moving forward to more recent times, on the national level an example for providing study and action is an issue that has become a source of trouble throughout the nation. In recent years, Violence Against Women or Domestic Violence Awareness, reached the point where it was legally defined and the Congress passed an Act that legislated against the growing problem. As already noted, in response to this "Call to Action" a District Court judge, Charles Flinn, was invited to speak to the Reading Room at its October 2009 meeting about the problems and the systems set up to work with abusive marriages in the courts.

There were other issues in recent years such as Americans with Disabilities, Family and Medical Leave, and legislation supporting hand-gun control. Study materials were available and local clubs throughout the country could implement activities they felt appropriate in their own towns or have local speakers address the problems in their communities.

The difference between former times and now is that the women not only heard a speaker relate the specific problems, but joined in a campaign to fight against them, or to educate a broader audience than just themselves. They didn't have a speaker just to hear about the issue, but to act on it.

In recent years a small group of newer members were known to discuss the proportion of dues sent to the GFWC. They could not understand any benefit that came from it. But the older members maintained loyalty to the long history of Reading Room membership in the state and national organizations and the stability they provided. They have always maintained an attitude of compliance with the organization that was set up so many years ago on the concept of a federation, something larger than a local club. This has maintained an order of tradition. The failure of some members to acknowledge this could simply be lack of communicating to new members its importance. Many of today's members feel that with the plethora of news and television specials, magazines and internet keep people abreast of the problems that might be addressed locally. It remains a fact that a concerted effort by many people standing together on an issue is more effective than one standing alone—whether the issue is local, national or international in scope.

ST. CLOUD READING ROOM FEDERATION MEMBER SINCE 1895.

The Reading Room became a charter member of the Minnesota Federation in 1895. It affiliated with the General Federation in 1906. As a member, the Society's organizational plan follows that of the Federation: A Constitution with laws and bylaws, the order of meeting, duties of the officers, the committees that are recommended by the Federation, and a stated purpose.

In the GFWC organization plan, the Education Department is dedicated to the advancement of Literacy and Lifelong Learning. This becomes important in the local group as an emphasis of their committee work. They will be open to study, discussion, and help in projects within their interests and expertise. The meetings operate under *Roberts Rules of Order* (Revised).

The meetings start with the club "collect," or prayer, the pledge of Allegiance, introduction of guests, secretary and

Yvonne Schilplin is given an award by the International GFWC president, Jackie Pierce. (Photo courtesy of Yvonne Schilplin)

treasurer reports, correspondence, discussion of old and new business, voting on any committee reports (the committee reports are five-minute announcements or reports of each committee), and, finally, the speaker for the meeting is introduced by the Program committee chairperson. Following the speaker, there is time for discussion, and then, dinner is served to the whole group, usually at the place of the meeting.

The committees adopted by the St. Cloud Reading Room Society follow:

Finance, Program, Entertainment, Civic, Conservation, Library, Nominating, Transportation, Publicity and Telephone, Filing (to be activated as needed), International Relations, Legislative, Federated News, Home Life, Special (ad hoc) which at this time, 2010, are a Special Library Funding Committee (Author Event), No Worry Books Project, and History of Reading Room Book, and By-laws. The Executive Committee is made up of officers of the Society.

CHAPTER SIX

Leadership of the Reading Room Society at Mid-Century

Mary Elizabeth Crandall Atwood, a leader in social, civic, club, educational and political circles in St. Cloud and Minnesota, served as Reading Room president in 1910-1911.

Mary Elizabeth Atwood was president of the Minnesota Federation of Women's Clubs and an active participant in educational, church, juvenile and suffrage work throughout the state. She was born in 1865 in Owatonna, Minnesota, the daughter of Hon. C.S. and Marietta Elizabeth Crandall. She attended public schools in Owatonna, and in 1882 graduated from the literary course of the Pillsbury Academy. She then attended Cornell University. After graduation, she became the principal of Preston Minnesota High School.

She came to St. Cloud where she became principal of the High School for three years, prior to her marriage to Clarence L. Atwood in 1890. Retired after marriage (as was typical at the time), she continued to be a valuable participant in educational work. As a member of the Board of Education, she introduced to the St. Cloud schools the most progressive educational ideas of the period. And on the Public Library board she was "equally valuable in giving the community at large the benefits of an exceptionally brilliant and well-trained mind." (From the Pioneer Society biography)

Mary Elizabeth was president of the St. Cloud Reading Room Society in 1904-1905 and 1905-1906. She also served as president of the Sorosis Club. In summer time, she assisted the Industrial School in seeing that school children received instruction in manual training and domestic science. She served on the board of the Unitarian Church as president of the board of trustees. With all of these activities in St. Cloud, however, she found time for civic work throughout the state— in the Suffragist Association, the Civics and Drama leagues, as well as committees on education and civics. She went beyond St. Cloud with her activities as an estimable member of the Minnesota Federation of Women's Clubs and served as its president during the years 1913 to 1915.

As president of the Minnesota Federation, she urged clubs to start rural clubs and said that the farm women were awakening to the spirit of progressiveness along with the industrial and literary lines. By 1913 to 1915, there were 270 clubs in Minnesota in 122 towns with a total of 16,120 members.

In her keynote speech to the GFWC at the annual meeting in Rochester on October 8, 1914, she spoke on the subject of "Peace." "OUR WORK FOR PEACE WILL NEVER END UNTIL IT GLADDENS THIS WORLD. It is for us to consecrate ourselves to it, to demand that textbooks for our children where the great sovereigns and wars of conquest are not extolled, where the constructive arts and sciences are given just recognition. . . . It is for women to study the question and mold public sentiment." Mary Elizabeth Atwood, October 8, 1914.

She was a delegate to the international conferences of Federated Women's Clubs. But she continued, always a person who was loyal to the work on the home front. To illustrate this, minutes of the May 13, 1919 meeting of Reading Room at her home were reported:

"Mrs. Atwood, chairman of Vacation School Committee reported the committee interviewing the board and finding them favorable to the idea of having such a school this summer, and they would pay $100 toward it and take charge of it, and that, owing to a lack of funds (the Vacation School), would accept the $50 from the Reading Room Society." The report was accepted.

Mrs. Atwood stated that the Society stands pledged to vacation schools and made a most eloquent plea that we continue our interest— and offer assistance. She made the motion that a committee be appointed to interview the board in regard to retaining Mr. Knudson to teach manual training. The motion was seconded and carried.

Mrs. Atwood had three sons, Crandall, Allen, and Fred C. She died on October 24, 1930, and was survived by her one daughter, Marjorie (Mrs. L. Hamilton) of St. Paul. Mr. Atwood and their three sons preceded Mrs. Atwood in death. The *St. Cloud Times* headed her obituary with the words: AN IDEAL CITIZEN.

Clarence L. Atwood, was born in 1859 in a small Illinois town. Later, his family moved to St. Cloud in time for him to enter the city high school, and he went on to St. Cloud State Normal School. With this preparation, he started teaching in Ramsey and Otter Tail counties. He then moved up to superintendent of schools at Melrose, where he remained for three years. He engaged in the real estate and mortgage loan business with his father, and, in 1902, Mr. Atwood organized the Security State Bank of St. Cloud and became its president. He was a member of the board of education for several years and was resident director of the St. Cloud State Normal School. He also served on the St. Cloud City Council for fifteen years. Atwood's great respect for St. Cloud State College continued into the next generation when his son, Allen Atwood, an attorney, his daughter, Mrs. Marjorie Hamilton, and Clarence himself were major benefactors for the Atwood Memorial College Center.

A great advance for St. Cloud was the purchase of the water works, which was accomplished and

Clarence Atwood, president of Security National Bank in 1902 and the leader of many organizations in the St. Cloud area. (Photo courtesy Stearns History Museum)

financed under Atwood's direction while he was chairman of the water works and fire protection committees of the council. He was a member of the Masons, the Elks, Modern Woodmen, and Royal Arcanum. His was a great life of service to the city.

MAUDE COLGROVE SCHILPLIN: A PROMINENT WRITER AND READING ROOM MEMBER AND PAST PRESIDENT

MAUDE SCHILPLIN, A PIONEER CLUBWOMAN and feature writer for the *St. Cloud Times*, was born in Charlotte, Michigan, March 29, 1871. She was the daughter of Charles H. Colgrove and Catherine Van Zile, descendants of Colonial and Revolution families. Maude was educated at Central High School in Minneapolis, and the University of Minnesota where she received her Baccalaureate in literature.

She was a high school teacher in St. Cloud from 1895 to 1898, until she married Frederick C. Schilplin on June 14, 1899, in St. Cloud. They had one son, the third Fred C. Schilplin.

She turned to feature writing at the *St. Cloud Daily Times*, the newspaper that her husband had purchased prior to their marriage. In 1929 she became secretary and treasurer of the Times Publishing Company where she had for nine years edited a daily column of "Worthwhile Verse" in that paper. The newspaper had become a joint family enterprise of some note throughout the state. Hers was the first poetry column in Minnesota and led to her writing the first *Anthology of Minnesota Verse*. For half a century she was helpmate to her husband and with him watched the *Times* grow from a modest journal to one of the leading newspapers in the northwest.

Maude was a member of many organizations, and in most of them she held office: The Twentieth Century Club in St. Cloud; vicepresident of the Minnesota Federation of Women's Clubs, and historian in 1941; a life member of the Minnesota Historical Society; National League of American Pen Women; and League of Minnesota Poets. In most organizations, she also held the position of historian, as she did in the St. Cloud Reading Room Society. She was president of the Reading Room in 1912-1913 and 1913-1914, and was named

Fred and Maude Schilplin at one more dinner on their busy schedule. (Photo courtesy *St. Cloud Times*)

Life Historian in 1935. The list of her activities and accomplishments is endless.

Beside all of these, according to the Minnesota Education Association (MEA) *Who's Who 1941*, she was deeply attached to her role as homemaker. The domestic arts were important in her life, and she was remembered for her gracious hospitality at her home at 395 Fifth Avenue South and at a summer home at Avon.

It was Maude Schilplin who wrote the historical account of the Reading Room that she was to read at the Golden Anniversary celebration in 1932. She had to miss the affair because of a death in the family. (No copy of this history could be found by this author, except for excerpts quoted in the Fiftieth Anniversary celebration newspaper article.)

Maude died on August 28, 1949, and is remembered as a devout Christian, state and community leader, loving wife and mother, and friend to the many people who knew her.

Maude's husband, Fred Schilplin, was born in Stearns County in 1868, the son of Lieutenant Frederick Schilplin-Eisle Kaiser, who for a short time published a German language newspaper. Fred was educated at St. Cloud Normal School, 1886-1887. He rose from apprentice on the *St. Cloud Times* in 1890 at age sixteen, and worked through all of the steps of newspapering to owner and publisher in 1906. He developed many related businesses as well as serving in public offices. In 1938 he built a radio station KFAM (K-Fred and Maude) operated by the Times Publishing Company. In the 1930s he developed "A Farm Beautiful." which was an experimental farm that also employed many people during that time of economic depression. Buildings from the farm still stand, visible from highway I-94. He held many offices in his newspaper profession as well as in local organizations. Fred Schilplin died April 28, 1949.

Fred Schilplin served the community well and will be remembered for his example of the "American Dream" fulfilled. His son, Frederick C. became the publisher of the *St. Cloud Times* after his father's death. He had a son, "Freddie," who did not follow the Freds who had gone before him. He, instead was interested in bicycle and car racing and established the American Bicycle Manufacturing Company in St. Cloud and followed his own bent. He married Yvonne Winter in 1947, and they had two sons, Frederick Phillip Winter Schilplin of Annandale and Chad Colgrove Winter Schilplin of Bloomington Minnesota.

M EMBERS OF THE ST. CLOUD Reading Room Society "felt a renewed and justifiable pride in their organization Thursday when the history of the society dramatized by Mrs. J.M. Dobson, was presented in the parlors of Lawrence Hall by a group of players dressed in some of the finery of pioneer days, garnered from the treasure chests of families whose life in St. Cloud dates back to the city's beginnings. The history of course recounts the efforts to organize and maintain a free reading room, which later developed into the public library"(*The Times*, March 15, 1935).

Use of a skit to present its history is a time-honored practice of the Society. This was one of the more eloquent ones, the work of Mrs. Dobson, who had written a short history of the Reading Room as well. The picture shows the women gathered on the stage of

Lawrence Hall after the presentation. The place was appropriate because Isabel Lawrence, a charter member of Reading Room, taught at
St. Cloud Normal School. The hall was named for her.

Reading Room members performed an historical skit written by Mrs. J.M. Dobson in the par-
lors of Lawrence Hall in 1935 and again in 1955. Members in the cast from left to right. (back
row) Mrs. R.B. Colbert, Mrs. C.B. Lewis, Mrs. J.I. Donahue, Mrs. William Freeman, Mrs.
Philip Halenbeck, Mrs. Thomas Donlin, Mrs. John Talbot, MRs. Julian McCutchan, Mrs. O.J.
Jerde, Mre. John H. Goven, Mrs. W.C. Croxton, Mrs. C.C. Dragoo, Mrs. W. Weber, Mrs.
Harry Clark, Mrs. Julius Buscher, Mrs. Charles Richter, Mrs. William Sartell. (front row) Mrs.
J.C. Cochran, Mrs. H.C. Bowing, Mrs. H.W. Goehrs, Miss Ellen Ready, Mrs. George A. Selke,
Mrs. B.T. Kemerer, Miss Isabelle Lawrence, Mrs. H.G. Young, Mres. W.B. Richards, Mrs.
Othmar Brick, Miss Marianne Clarke, Mres. H.B. Gough, Mrs. J.M. Dobson, Mrs. L.D. Zeleny,
Mrs. Allen Atwood. (Photo courtesy of the Reading Room Society Archives)

CHAPTER SEVEN

1945 to 1975
Changes and a New Library

With the end of World War II in 1945, life started to resume its former pace, and the economy took an upward turn. Normalcy was restored. The St. Cloud librarian at the time of her annual report pointed to the library's place in the postwar world:

"World War II and the coming of the atomic power have emphasized the interdependence of all nations. The greatest necessity today is for the world's people to be informed about one another's ways, thoughts and hope. The public library recognizing no bars of wealth, class or creed, and aiming to present all sides of controversial issues, can help to obliterate ignorance, prejudice and misunderstandings" (Mrs. Merle Lennartson, head librarian and member of the Reading Room).

The committee reports of the meeting of the Society in November 1947 provided a feeling of a more peaceful time: "It was announced that Morgan Price Jones, an exchange teacher from England on the Technical High School faculty, would be the speaker at the November 20 meeting."

The Reading Room endorsed a letter presented by the Civic Committee to be sent to the City Council asking for more adequate lighting in residential neighborhoods of St. Cloud. Other committee reports

The old Nehemiah Clarke residence continues to grace the neighborhood on Third Avenue South. (Photo courtesy of the *St. Cloud Times*)

included statements regarding an Audubon tour at the Teachers College, Girl Scout leaders and Council members' plans to send CARE packages to Europe before Christmas, a call for magazines for the Veterans Administration Hospital, and an historical exhibit at the public library.

The speaker was Walter Rogosheske, a member of the Legislature Research Committee, who explained to Reading Room members the aims, methods, and needs of the group he represented. This committee was authorized to study subjects that would come up for consideration in the next legislative session. He explained how this study worked and how the findings were applied to the items that had been considered.

Mrs. Fred Schilplin was honored with a memorial: A Minnesota writers' collection was begun at the library, as reported in the *St. Cloud Daily Times* of September 13, 1949: "To honor the late Mrs. Fred Schilplin, its first historian, the League of Minnesota Poets has voted to establish a Maude Colgrove Schilplin shelf in the St. Cloud Public Library. This shelf will include volumes by Minnesota writers present and past."

The St. Cloud Library moved into the modern postwar era with new services available by the 1950s. A "Recordak" microfilm reader was installed in 1951; in 1952, the library began a film service for community group leaders with the Film Council of America. Reading programs were sponsored by the library with children from elementary schools, and the Mad Hatter Reading Club was organized to foster interest in books of juvenile literature.

In 1952 the annual library report for its fiftieth year would claim 156,967 books circulated.

On November 14, 1952, the St. Cloud Library marked its fiftieth anniversary with an open house in the afternoon and evening. The whole city was invited to attend.

"Recognition must be given to the St. Cloud Reading Room Society which brought the library project into reality many years ago, and sponsored a library movement in this community about three quarters of a century ago.

"Every year the Reading Room Society provides a handsome gift for the library here, and its influence in it has been tremendously

The 1952 Annual Meeting took place at Mrs. Charles Richter's home at Highbanks on the Mississippi River. Left to right: Mrs. H.B. Gough, Mrs. H.C. Bowing, Mrs. John H. Boven, Mrs. W.W. Holes, Mrs. Colie Guy, Mrs. Frank E. Murphy, Mrs. Harry W. Cater, Mrs. Tom Donlin, Mrs. F.E. Perkins, Mrs. A.J. Tschumperlin, Mrs. Merle Lennartson, Mrs. C. Morrison, Mrs. D.H. Knickerbacker, Mrs. Gilman Goehrs, Mrs. H.W. Goehrs, Mrs. Allen A. Atwood, Mrs. J.M. Dobson, Mrs. R.T. Peterson, Mrs. Emil Maizner, Mrs. Dickens Lewis, Mrs. Albert Strobel, Miss Lydia Gorman, Mrs. Tom Sartell, Mrs. L.M. Evans, Mrs. J.C. Buscher, Mrs. W.A. LaRocque, Mrs. C.B Lewis, and Mrs. Charles Richter. (Photo courtesy of the Reading Room Society Archives)

effective all this period" (Harold Scholkopf, *St. Cloud Daily Times*, November 14, 1952).

Mrs. Tschumperlin, Society historian, noted in 1940 in a summary of Reading Room financial gifts to the library that in its sixty years, 1880 to 1940, "Reading Room society had contributed $25,000, equaling the gift of Mr. Carnegie, but in no wise belittling it."

"Just a Note: At a meeting during the seventy-fifth anniversary year, 1957, Mrs. Rosenberger commended the monthly reminiscences given by the daughters of the past ten presidents—and the privilege of having an international delegate, Mrs. Dobson at the Geneva meeting."

At home a plan for beautifying roads was studied: In the early 1960s, a time when highway rebuilding and repair was moving toward the national freeway system, members of the St. Cloud Reading Room met at Mrs. Leonard Williams's house to discuss the roadside approaches to St. Cloud. Representatives of several city organizations met to discuss the Roadside Development Committee of the Federation of Women's Clubs, whose goal was to enhance the appearance of the state for tourists through roadside improvement and beautification. Representing the Reading Room Society were Mrs. C.B. Lewis, Mrs. H.B. Gough, Mrs. J.H. Goven, and Mrs. L.A. Williams. Other members were representatives of the Twentieth Century Club, the American Legion Auxilliary, Sorosis, the State Reformatory, mayors of Sauk Rapids and St. Cloud, Junior Chamber of Commerce, and Frank Kindler, florist and nurseryman.

Mrs. Williams chose a committee of three to investigate the possibilities for this season and to bring its recommendations to a later meeting. The project, to beautify the roads as they enter the city, was in keeping with St. Cloud's reputation as the cleanest city in the state. Mrs. Williams, the hostess, assisted by Mrs. C.B. Lewis and Mrs. H.C. Bowing, "served delightful refreshments at a social after the business meeting" (*St. Cloud Times* undated article).

1965 VOTE ON PRELIMINARY PLANS FOR A NEW LIBRARY.

So CERTAIN WAS THE EXPECTED APPROVAL of the voters, the architects were selected to draw up preliminary plans for a new library on land designated at Fourth Avenue South and St. Germain. But, the 1965 vote on the bond issue was hotly contested and the NO votes won, a great disappointment to many people. The new library proposition scored 3,433 YES votes to 2,295 NO votes, but, since it required a five-eighths vote in favor, or 3,607 votes for passage, the proposition failed. The defeat was very painful for those who saw the need for a new, larger and updated library. It was voted down again in a second election the same year.

"On the brighter side, it was the year in which we received our first Federal Grant for books and other library materials. Hope for a new library continues though dimmed momentarily." Mrs. Lennartson, Librarian.

In 1964 another large gift came from the estate of Jessie Smith, prominent Reading Room member. The Society organized the sale of her furnishings, and the money was placed in a special account to be used as a Jesse Smith Memorial fund in the new library when it finally was built.

St. Cloud grew into a larger center with many new inhabitants each year and continuing expansion in industry. Along with the growth appeared many new activities and associations that, like the Reading Room Society, wished to add to the cultural and educational level of the city. This interest was demonstrated in gifts at that time from the American Association of University Women of a collection of paintings to be used as a future circulating art collection. The Unitarian Fellowship presented a woodcut by William Ellingson, noted artist at St. Cloud State College.

St. Cloud was no longer a small town: the 1960 population was 33,815 having grown from 9,500 in 1900; 24,000 in 1930. By this time the library was operating with advanced technology, new methods of operation, and different kinds of books needed by an increasingly diverse population. None of

YOUR LIBRARY NEEDS YOUR YES VOTE MAY 4TH, 1965

this could have been imagined by the people involved in the opening of the Carnegie Library in 1902. The increased population provided increased tax revenue available for the library. Government grants, formerly unknown, were available for libraries, for books, buildings and services, especially in rural areas.

PLANNING PROCESS FOR A REGIONAL LIBRARY SYSTEM GROWS

By 1959, A GREAT DEAL OF STUDY and work had commenced in the planning of a regional library system that would reach outside St. Cloud. In 1969 the process of planning came to completion and a six-county Great River Library Association was a reality. It was accepted by commissioners of Benton, Morrison, Sherburne, Stearns, Todd, and Wright counties and by the St. Cloud City Council, each with a representative on the Regional Library Board. St. Cloud Library was designated headquarters of this enlarged system. The thirteen branches included in the system covered a population that added up to some 206,000, an indication of the scope of the library system that was about to come into place. The new library building was not yet built. In 1968,

Handing over the deed of the library. Mayor Edward Henry, Mrs. Joseph Laughlin, president, Mrs. Edward Weber, Mrs. Grace McDowall, Mrs. Tom Donlin, Mrs. Kurt Stai, Mrs. Harry Gough, Mrs. Charles Richeter, Mrs. John Goven, Mrs. James Dobson, Mrs. Floyd Perkins, Mrs. Frank E. Murphy, Mrs. W.B. Richards, Mrs. C.B. Lewis, and Mrs. Allen Atwood. (Photo courtesy *St. Cloud Times*)

the St. Cloud Library had 68,755 books with a circulation of 242,166, illustrating the need for expanded facilities.

The struggle for the bond issue had gone on for a dozen years. The Reading Room women decided they needed more help. They, along with Sorosis and AAUW, en-

Friends of the Library Organization: John Bensen, Mrs. Chester Otto, Mrs. Warren Hutchens, Frederick Fandel, and St. Inez Hilger, OSB. (Photo courtesy Stearns History Museum)

Tree-Hugging Pioneers. This cartoon appeared on the January 1902 cover of *The Courant*, which included a banner declaring the issue was "addressed officially by the clubwomen to the business men of the Northwest."

listed the help of the newly organized Friends of the Library, and all joined together in the effort.

Amelia Bowing, sixty-five-year member of the Reading Room, accomplished great work in conservation of natural resources throughout Minnesota. She was president of the Society, 1927 to 1929.

READING ROOM MEMBER FOR SIXTY-FIVE YEARS WINS high praise for her work as Conservation Leader from Glanville Smith, well-known

Writer and Raconteur. Amelia Bowing was born in Spring Valley, Minnesota, in 1869 to Henry W. and Elizabeth Hockema. She married Mr. H.C. Bowing of St. Cloud, Minnesota, August 17, 1898. Amelia was educated in Minnesota public schools, attended Teachers College in Winona, Minnesota, and taught in public Schools in St. Cloud from 1893 to 1897. She retired to marry Mr. Bowing, and they had one daughter, Elizabeth, who became a librarian (The *St. Cloud Daily Times*, April 13, 1964). Excerpts from talk by Glanville Smith: Sixty-five years of membership in an organization is an exceptional record. Such a record has been attained this year by Mrs. H.C. Bowing. St. Cloud's Reading Room Society is the organization of which she has been a member since 1899—sixty-five years.

"Mrs. Bowing, now in honorary status, for half century was an active member. She served as secretary, vice-president, and as president, but earned a unique place in the club's history as its Conservation chairman, an opportunity to exert influence in a field that she heartily regarded as important. The Reading Room Society's Conservation chairman soon found herself chairman for the entire Minnesota Federation of Women's Clubs. And before the eleven years of her state-wide service were at an end she had had the satisfaction of seeing a thousand-acre reforestation project carried through by the Federation. This was the chief tangible memento of Mrs. Bowing's zeal, but there were other achievements along the way.

"One was with Federation urging, a series of attractive pamphlets distributed to the schools by the State Conservation Department. Of the committee of five appointed by the governor to push this project through, Mrs. Bowing was the only woman. From these pamphlets, Minnesota youngsters imbibed information and attitudes toward woods and waters, bird life and forest fires. She promoted popular bus caravans which swept the ladies from the capital in St. Paul to fish hatcheries, primeval woods, CCC camps, even free nurseries and burgeoning resort areas in the north.

"There were rich friendships among club women who shared her views and those of state and federal executives. They found that here was a botanist with whom they could bandy scientific data.

"Mrs. Bowing's earliest years in the Reading Room Society saw the great task achieved of providing St. Cloud with a public library. In this she played an ardent part, as she had also in the city's book-review club, Sorosis. Parallel to club duties had been Mrs. Bowing's long service to her Presbyterian church, where she participated in its Deaconess committee.

"At the same time, there had been a life of hospitality, both in town and at the Pleasant Lake cottage. Her husband, H.C. Bowing, was, in his lifetime, one of the city's chief grocers: Bowing Brothers was the gastronome's headquarters. This assured first-class resources for Bowing picnics."

More about Mrs. Bowing's work with reforestation of the Superior National Forest from the Federation Archives: When Calvin Coolidge established a Bicentennial Commission to celebrate the 200th anniversary of George Washington's birth, the General Federation of Clubs was first to be called on for help. Mrs. Bowing, chair of the Minnesota Federation, sent a "call to action" to all member organizations to join the effort.

The Minnesota group was responsible for one thousand acres, called "The Federation Forest." Individuals were encouraged to pay $5.00 to plant 1,000 trees in an acre. The trees were provided by the U.S. Forest Service; the cost of planting was $5.00. The Federation Forest is 1,000 acres within the Superior National Forest on the Ely-Finland Road that was reforested by the Women's Clubs.

Earlier, in 1900, the Minnesota Federation had made a name for itself. "In Minnesota, no single organization was more active than the group in promoting scientific forestry and the nascent conservation movement. The Federation's early members demonstrated progressive thinking and a capacity for stirring controversy. With leaders like Maria Sanford, University of Minnesota professor of rhetoric, and Margaret Evans, principal of Carlton College and the Federation's first president, the group was viewed by the popular press as the 'Brainy Women of Minnesota'" (Tim Brady, *Minnesota Conservation Volunteer Magazine*).

CHAPTER EIGHT

Reading Room Looks at Its Mission Anew

The new library opened October 14, 1979, on St. Germain and Fourth Avenue. The Carnegie Library was demolished in 1982, eighty years after its opening. The new building, designed by Duane Thorber of Interdesign Inc., an architectural firm, was built by Donlar Corporation. It was planned and built to accommodate a much larger collection of books, a memorable children's library, and the technological advances of the time. It was celebrated by book lovers who had struggled for several years to have its construction approved by the city since it was first put to a vote in 1965. In 1980, Genevieve Flanagan, president during the building of the new library, gave her annual report to the membership as her term came to a close. The centennial year of the Society was 1980.

"I am sure that our beautiful centennial celebration has been good for all of us, truly an inspiration, for within us we carry the spirit and devotion to Reading Room, and hopefully, will perpetuate it from generation to generation. My thanks to Mary F. Peterson and all of you members who made this centennial celebration one to remember. Our Mrs. Goven in her excerpts from the past has kept us attuned to our heritage.

"At the dedication of our new three million dollar library, Reading Room contributed a total of $7,000. [A total of] $1,245 was

Genevieve Flanagan, president of the Reading Room during the building of the new library in 1979 and in the centennial year (1980) of the Reading Room Society.

donated by our present members with contributions ranging from twenty dollars to $100. Five thousand dollars represents interest on savings through the years. While Reading Room contributed this amount, at the Dedication we still hold the $7,000 in savings. It is for works of Art. There is a standing committee to assure continuity: Gloria Laughlin, Margaret Henning, Mary Baker, Priscilla Weber, and Merle Lennartson."

After the opening of the new library, Friends of the Library, as noted earlier, assumed a greater supportive role at the library. The members of that group became increasingly active as they studied the areas in which they might be of help to the library. They worked as volunteers in the library, shelving books and other tasks to help the professional staff; they also organized the collection and sale of used books in a room set aside for this project. The new Friends organization president reported to the library. The president of the Friends of the Library in 2009-2010 was Jo Marie (Mrs. Dennis Weis).

Then, as the Great River Library network grew, the fine "new" library began to outgrow its space. It had become the headquarters for the six-county system, each county with a representative on the Regional Library Board. Thirty-two libraries in the system shared the same large collection of books, videotapes, DVDs, music, and compact discs, and other items. But, the demands placed on the 1979 library

Drawing of the second library, used for publicity.

with the growth of the regional system became too great and the needs of the community were not being adequately served. Plus, a shortage of parking space prevented many people from using the facility.

At the same time, the St. Cloud Civic Center was more frequently unable to accommodate many exhibits, shows, and conventions because its facilities were not large enough. This resulted in a growing advocacy to provide expanded exhibit and meeting space. A whole new center was financially out of the question. But, how to expand the present building? The response—the proposal to add thousands of feet of additional space by moving westward across Fourth Avenue—and using the space occupied by the library. The library would have to be the one to move . . . first.

CHAPTER NINE

The First Ten Years of the Twenty-First Century

Aforward-thinking Yvonne Schilplin brought the Reading Room Society into the twenty-first century as president during her years, 1998 to 2000. She was General Federation of Women's Clubs of Minnesota president, and has served as president of numerous other offices and committees. She currently serves as president of the Annandale chapter of the GFWC, which she established in 2003. She has been the editor and publisher of the *Loon E News* an on-line GFWC newsletter, and she oversaw the implementation of the GFWC of Minnesota website. She serves on the International Board of Directors as 2008 to 2010 Strategic Planning Committee member.

Yvonne is listed in *Who's Who of American Women* and *A Tribute to Outstanding Minnesota Women*. She was a recipient of the 1994 Minnesota School Board State Leadership Award, served as chairman of the Annandale School Board, Education chair of the Minnesota PTA, and many more important roles. In 1999 she became a charter member of the St. John's Preparatory School Council and most recently (May 2010) was named member of the St. John's Prep Board of Regents. This is only a scan of her achievements, but, really . . . !

Having grown through the ranks of the General Federation of Women's Clubs on international, national, state and local levels, she

Yvonne Schilplin, 1998 to 2000 Reading Room president. (Photo courtesy Reading Room Archives)

brought that enthusiasm to her presidency of Reading Room. She made the Society aware of the larger group to which it associated and the need for understanding the place of St. Cloud in its plan. She reported carefully on the activities and ideas of the Federation during her presidency, but because there had been a lapse in this interest, it would take some time to convince the group of the importance of the national level of the GFWC and its influence on many of the projects throughout their local history.

It was with strength of spirit and attitude that she guided the St. Cloud Reading Room through her two years and continues to manifest it as an active member and Chairman of the History Committee.

In 2010 a "President Survey" was developed. To the questions asked, respondents could respond by answering the questions as they were given; they could choose which ones they wished to reply to or write a paragraph as they wished.

1. What was your main goal at the beginning of your term as president? Did you feel you accomplished it?

2. What did you see as Reading Room's chief activity or purpose?

3. What changes came about during your presidency?

4. Do you think the Reading Room is heading in a new direction for the future?

Following are Yvonne's answers to the survey:

"1. Goal: Recruit ten new members . . . which conveyed, smiles, stares, and mumbles from the members as this daunting goal brought forth the traditions that don't allow for ease of recruiting new members—only one new member per year per member and only if you were a member in 'good standing' for a year, vouchers from five members, ballots, and, at the time, limits on number of members. The goal was realized and as a result our club was recognized in the *GFCW International Headquarters Magazine*.

"2. Recognize all members—Members donned hats in a 'Hats Off to Women' celebration at the annual meeting, culminating with recognition of Gen Flanagan as a fifty-year member of the Society and honored Life members, Gloria Laughlin and Priscilla Weber. The club celebrated 120 years of volunteer service, receiving a certificate of appreciation from GFWC International. Orientation for new members was held during the year.

Past president celebration group photo. Blanch Carlson, 1988-1990, Ann Didier, 1991-1992, Beulah Rose Hutchens, 1986-1988, Bernice Landy, 1974-1976, Margaret Kline, 1994-1996, Gen Flanagan, 1978-1980 and 1981-1982, Gloria Laughlin, 1964-1966, Rachel Vesser, 1996-1998, with outgoing president Yvonne Schilplin, 1998-2000.

Karen Vann, president of the Reading Room Society from 2000 to 2002. (Photo courtesy of the Reading Room Archives)

"3. Promote a much needed connection of members to GFWC. Video included a message from the international president and other presentations by Minnesota officers resulted in an increase in attendance by club delegates to GFWC conventions and workshops.

"It was a privilege and an honor to have served as president of this illustrious group of 'ladies.' When asked about the future, one must remain optimistic of the endless possibilities afforded us to make positive changes in our communities and our world. Our club must continue to be a valued and committed community service organization."

KAREN VANN SERVED AS PRESIDENT DURING 2000 TO 2002.

THE GENERAL FEDERATION THEME WAS A Rainbow of Women's Ideas and Interests: "We expanded the theme to include a Rainbow of Service—celebrating volunteerism and the many ways our membership had been active in service to the community. We learned that collectively our members had volunteered for 109 different agencies and/or not-for-profit organizations.

"The 2001-2002 theme was 'Pathways.' During that year, we were beginning to realize that the 'pathway' to attracting new members and being a viable organization was scattered with pitfalls. It became necessary to look at our traditions and practices to assess how well they were meeting the needs of today's women. We learned that some new 'pathways' must be developed.

"In the subsequent ten years, a number of changes have been made to clear the 'pathway.'"

• Hostesses for each meeting no longer pay for all of the meals. Instead members pay for their own meals. Hostesses still select the location of the meeting, decorate the tables, and determine menu.

• We amended by-laws to accommodate a larger membership.

• Attire is no longer limited to dresses or skirts, but rather all business attire is appropriate at meetings.

• We changed the months in which we meet—substituting April and June meetings for February and March—to accommodate those who winter in the South.

• We streamlined the method of invitation to membership.

• We received 501(c)3 status with the Internal Revenue Service, which allows donors to deduct contributions to our Society on their income tax.

We continue to keep the Great River Regional Library as our primary philanthropy. However, literacy of children in the St. Cloud area has been added as a focus for our membership. Establishing the No Worry Book program has helped to address that concern.

Although the process has been arduous, I believe we are moving in the direction of becoming a society of the twenty-first century while continuing to honor the contributions of the hundreds of St.Cloud Reading Room Society women who have preceded us."

JOAN TEIGEN, PRESIDENT DURING 2003.

1. "I ACTUALLY HAD TWO GOALS. We needed to attract more members. Our membership was aging, and I felt we needed to get some more enthusiasm and energy to bring it in sync with the world of today.

"We needed to make some changes. One change, which was controversial, was to pay for our own meals at each meeting instead of paying for all meals every time our turn came. There was some discussion over a couple of meetings, pro and con. The change was ultimatel voted in and continues to be acceptable.

2 "I struggled with this one. (Activity or purpose) We do not seem to be recognized in our community. After going through hours in the archives (which are wonderful and very complete), I feel we have not done a proper job of keeping an identity. We need a united goal and evaluation process. As I went through my first months of presidency, I was awed

Joan Teigen, president 2003. (Photo courtesy of the Reading Room Archives)

(and still am) by the talent, active lives, and graciousness of this group of women. I felt the opportunity to be part of this group was an honor. I also felt we needed more of a focus as a group. The programs were and are still excellent and educational. The dinner is a wonderful time for socialization, which is important.

"The business meeting was orderly but lacked a general purpose. I felt some of the committees should be eliminated as there was not time at each meeting to do them justice. They need to be reevaluated. We need to take a hard look at them and determine which are really worthwhile and those of little interest; then decide which should be dropped.

3. "The addition of new members has brought new life and ideas into the organization. I think the women are becoming more involved in leadership positions and not as constrained by rigid protocol to speak up.

"I recognize that there is resistance to change, which at times inhibits new endeavors. I also think paying for their own meals makes it easier for members to budget their expenses.

4. "Reading Room has to head in a new direction in some areas. Today's women have many more demands on their time. We have to have concrete goals/visions to attract them. I think the leaders of organization need to articulate a clear vision in writing that describes what they want to accomplish and how to achieve it.

Ideally all members should participate. This should be explained as an expectation of membership. This vision should clearly depict how the achievement of this vision will improve our organization. We have to then believe it is relevant and realistic. It needs to be promising. We don't need so many committees, but active ones.

"Part of this needs to be done by each president and her board. At the end of the year this vision or goal needs to be evaluated as to whether it is successful or not. It should then be followed by a report, or suggestions need to be made for the following year. We should not be afraid of failure but feel good about our successes. Our committees should be evaluated. Some are obsolete."

Left to right: Erika Aschman, Kirsty Smith, Constance Crane. Reading Room Celebrates 125 years. (Photo by Pat Witte.)

Constance Crane, president from 2004-2005. (Photo by Pat Witte)

M. Constance Crane, President 2004-2006

Constance is a retired Tech High School English teacher and now a world traveler who has taken a very active role in Reading Room for many years. Following are her thoughts on her years in office:

"I have seen some new areas being developed such as the No-Worry Books project, the Author's Night, and this last two years' excitement about the successful publishing and marketing of the history book. These are all new projects, and are exactly what we need. If we continue in this mode, Reading Room will survive and be a vital and necessary part of our community."

Barbara Saigo turns the gavel over to newly elected president Marilyn Obermiller in 2009. (Photo by Pat Witte)

For 2005-2006 "As an organization with its foundation in meeting the library needs of the community, the Reading Room Society theme was "Learning Never Ends." We continued to be library advocates and served on various committees for the building of the new library. Reading Room directed us to support literacy programs at the library and in the community. Nancy Hubbard led us toward what would become the "Gently Used Books" project.

In 2006-2007: "Even though we are in the twenty-first century, we women still need to recognize how important it is to help other women. The Reading Room Society examines women's issues through its programs at each meeting and works on achieving the year's goal of 'Empowering Women.'"

Barbara Saigo, Ph.D., came to St. Cloud when her husband was named president of St. Cloud State University. She of course became involved in the life of the campus, but having heard of the Reading Room from some friends, she became a member in 2001.

She was elected president in 2007-2008 and 2008-2009. At the end of her term, she was able to make the following talk to the Society's last meeting, summarizing her two years in office:

St. Cloud Reading Room Society, 2005. Left to right, back row: Maurine Unger, Helen Catton, June Kelly, Ann Didier, Mary Lou Burns, Irene Frank, Louisa Johnson, Gloria Laughlin, Yvonne Kramer, Marilyn Obermiller, Karen Pederson, Corrine Janochoski, Pat Zenner, Joan Teigen, Constance Crane; middle row: Carol Hilger, Rachael Veeser, Kay Heinen, Marilyn Ames, Kelly Wischmann, Nancy Hubbard, Pat Witte, Joan Kowalkowski, Marge Teague, Beulah Rose Hutchens, Norma Erickson, Karen Vann, Bobbie Bright; front row: Connie Sanvick, Geri Galaneault, Mary Sommers, and Barbara Saigo. (Photo courtesy of the Camera Shop.)

"For 2008-2009 I chose the theme "Vitality," representing the energy, vigor, and wealth of ideas ad experience of our members, both individually and collectively. Wow! What you have done with your talents and energy!

Collected and distributed more than 10,000 No-Worry books, with that project recognized at the GFWC state level.

Committed $15,000 to the new library for a named room.

Donated and conducted fund-raising activities to meet our pledge, including two author events.

Participated in library planning, events, and celebrations.

Although we lost a few members, we have gained vital new members—eleven in just this year.

Started an Epsilon Sigma Omicron ESO book group.

Achieved 501(c)3 tax status—retroactive to March 14, 1882!

Updated and re-filed our Articles and Bylaws with the State of Minnesota.

Caught up on our reporting to the State of Minnesota.

(Now that these three changes have been completed, we are finally ready to print the Articles and Bylaws as a pocket booklet for members to keep with their annual Yearbook.)

Provided direct support to worthy community organizations, with gifts, donations, and volunteer time through our Home Life Committee.

Had our Pat Zenner selected for the Minnesota Empowered Woman award.

Started an Oral History Project, beginning with the oldest members.

Began the History of Reading Room Project, which will culminate in publication and distribution of a book.

"I deliberately ended with the history projects because I want to read to you an email from International GFWC President Rose Ditto, on May 12, 2009.

"'Good afternoon, Barbara! I want to congratulate you and your GFWC St. Cloud Reading Room Society members on winning

Nancy Hubbard, chair of No Worry Books, Bobbie Bright, Book Committee and Reading Room historian. (Photo by Pat Witte)

Marilyn Obermiller, president 2009-2010, and going into 2011. (Photo by Robert Obermiller)

the overall club award for the Women's History and Resource Center area. There are six categories and states in those categories receive certificates, but your club receives the overall award of $50.00.'"

And now to the 130th year of Reading Room under the leadership of Marilyn Gilbride (Mrs. Robert) Obermiller!

Marilyn was born and raised in Pierz, Minnesota, and married Robert Obermiller, They have had three children, and have lived in Milwaukee, Bloomington, Indiana, and St. Cloud. She became a Registered Nurse at the St. Cloud Hospital School of Nursing in 1956, received the B.E.S. Major-Speech Communication at St. Cloud State University; and a degree of Administrator of Volunteers, a Professional Development Program, from Metropolitan State University, Minneapolis, in 1986. She was employed as an RN by the St. Cloud Hospital and the Veterans' Hospital, Milwaukee, Wisconsin.

At St. Cloud Hospital, she was coordinator of Development of the Hospice Volunteer Program and a Hospice Volunteer for Approximately twenty years. Marilyn has served in leadership positions in several arts-related organizations: The Annual May Bowle—a three-college fund raiser in the 1970s—St. Cloud Community Arts Council Board, County Stearns Theatrical Company Board, Citizens for the Arts, United Arts of Central Minnesota, Friends of the Minneapolis Institute of Art. She has served on community boards: Central Health Foundation as V.P. three years, then president for another three, as well as Community Collaboration, Central Minnesota Community Foundation Women's Fund Advisory Board, Memory Care Clinic, Friends of Munsinger/ Clemens Gardens Advisory Board, St. Cloud Reading Room Society chair 2009 to 2011.

Reading the comments of a representative group of presidents of the twenty-first century, makes it clear that Marilyn is serving at a crucial time. We can see that the women we have heard from have acknowledged problems and difficulties during the past ten years and made positive attempts to solve them.

COMMENTS ON BEING A READING ROOM SOCIETY PRESIDENT
MARILYN OBERMILLER, 2009-2011

"IT IS SAID THAT WE STAND on the shoulders of those who came before us. This lofty place from which we see is not just a perch, but a gift that comes with responsibility. It must count for something.

"When I accepted the role of president, my focus was on evaluating the organization, building on our strengths and traditions, honoring our older members *and* redefining how our club and members function. We cannot go forward without knowing the roads that women walk *today*.

"New members will not join us unless what we offer them is relevant to their lives. Their time is precious, stretched between work and family. Yet their needs today, as with women before, will be balanced to include comradeship with other women, having the opportunity to learn new things and of course have some fun.

"Alice Walker said, 'Women have to summon up courage to fulfill dormant dreams.' We would do well to carry our history with us but we must walk down our own road."

CHAPTER TEN

Reading Room Looks Back, and Moves Forward

S o, enters the "New" New Library on Twelfth Avenue and St. Germain, designed by GLT Architectural firm, and built by Donlin Contractors. But this is now the library story, not the Reading Room story. Perhaps the Society's story must continue into a future of its own.

The Reading Room could not live or re-live its past, nor could it forget its commitment to the wonderful women who went before them. It became a time of redefining the work of the Society. Continuing its interest in the library, its activities and needs, it also continued activities that promoted reading and culture among its members and the community.

The Society's help was no longer a necessity for funding and helping solve problems of the large Great River Regional Library system which the St. Cloud Library had

Alice Wick, honorary chair of the Library Capital Campaign. (Photo courtesy Stearns History Museum)

111

The new Great River Regional Library opened in 2008. (Photo by Pat Witte)

become in one hundred and twenty-five plus years. The librarian had always been a member of Reading Room and continued to report on the ongoing work and activities of the new library system, and the Society never wavered in its support and interest in the library. During the final year of the NEW library project, the Society was kept informed with plans and progress reports from the city librarian. The Society also viewed the building plans for the new structure and pictures of the coming edifice as it advanced. Members participated in the festivities of the opening days.

Reading Room continues with its commitment of the very early years to being a social as well as cultural group. It also continues long-cherished practices of asking members to pay ten dollars in addition to their annual dues as a fund for the library to buy books as memorials on the death of a member. Reading Room continues to send advocacy letters—for example, to the City Council, the mayor's office, the Library Board—when necessary to promote their point of view on the needs of the library and other matters that arise in the city and that they can endorse.

A Beginning of Changes in the Society's Focus.

A NEW MONEY-MAKING VENTURE WAS initiated to raise money as a gift to St. Cloud's new library to provide a room named "The Reading Room." The "Author Event," chaired by Constance Crane, is currently moving towards its third year, a money-raiser, but also a way to allow local authors to introduce their works to the general public. The speaker is followed by discussion with the author, and with coffee and dessert. Hopefully, it will continue, as an annual, or even a more frequent, event.

As previously noted, four members contacted older members to interview them for first hand memories of their active days in the Reading Room Society. These are recorded on compact discs and have been added to the archives of the Society. The interviewers were Constance Crane, Helen Catton, Erika Aschmann and Beulah Rose Hutchens.

At the first meeting in 2009 Kirsty Smith, director of Great River Library, announced that the library needed volunteers to provide story telling sessions to pre-school children. This would be a one-day-a-week commitment after the women have been trained by professional teachers in the techniques of the task. Ten women accepted the offer to join the program on a trial basis. It was tentatively added to ascertain its acceptance by families and schools. However, participation by children was limited and the activity was discontinued.

In another area of service, member Pat Zenner has for many years been active with the March of Dimes support for the health of newborn babies. Each year she heads up a Baby Shower

Kirsty Smith, director of the Great River Regional Library, and a member of the Reading Room Society.

"No Worry" books workers sort books in a members garage. Left to right: Vonnie Bangston, Norrie Mahowald, Mary Tasto, Connie Crane, Yvonne Schilplin, Donna Radeke, and Bonnie Hall. (Photo courtesy of the Reading Room Society Archives)

for Reading Room's participation. Members bring supplies for new-born infants, items of all kinds that are needed. Pat has served as national representative on the GFWC. She has been honored with many awards for volunteerism. She was given the national award, cited for "Daily Points of Light" by President Bush who stated, "I applaud your dedication to help others . . . to transform our Nation one heart at a time." In 2010 she was honored for thirty years with the March of Dimes.

Inspired by a talk on the specific needs of schools with large numbers of children of low income families, another Society member started the "No Worry Books" project to collect books for schools with a high proportion of families unable to purchase books. These books were placed in the schools' libraries. The children could then select their own to keep. This activity became very popular and drew several women to help in the project. An ad hoc committee was formed and has become a working committee in the St. Cloud Reading Room. Seven thousand books have been distributed in the first three years of the program; in 2010, the total books reached 25,000. The choice of schools and delivery of books is coordinated with the St. Cloud Public School System. A representative elementary teacher from one of the schools receiving this aid spoke to the Society to describe the delighted reception by the children who are given books and the great success of the program. Vigorously heading this activity has been Nancy Hubbard.

As a way to bring the membership into the history study, a special program was written by the author of this book. Performed by members of the History Committee, a skit depicted the early days in St. Cloud when, in the 1870s a homesick young woman wrote home to tell her family about life here in St. Cloud and the friends she had met. She described their meeting as the "Library Association" and approaching the city fathers about the hopes of their society to one day provide a free reading room and public library for the citizens. This was a fictitious letter, but it was an historical account of those first years when living was hard and a young woman was homesick for the civilization in the old Vermont town from which she came to this outpost on the Mississippi River. The actors in the skit went on to communicate with their families over the years using new modes of communication. They drew some laughs as they "reported" by telegraph, old-style phone and to the present, by cell phone and email as they moved from past to present times.

At dinner following that meeting, a questionnaire was distributed, asking members for their comments and ideas on organizational changes, new programs, or the conduct of meetings. The members attending—and several guests—enjoyed the program. More were planned. However, little response was shown to the questionnaire.

These activities are the beginning of new life in an old organization. The Reading Room has been inspired by looking back to the people who founded their organization. Now, in 2010, at 130 years, the Society remembers and honors its past history. It is proud to have inherited the tradition of the many strong women who were effective advocates and builders of the library system, the beautiful park system, the cleanliness of the streets, ordinances regarding food handling, development of the early school system, and so many other activities that were promoted by the women of Reading Room. They provided resources during difficult periods as our city grew from its earliest days. In a new era when the public provides for educational resources and outstanding library system, Reading Room will continue to support those interests, but in new ways.

The Indomitable Ladies come to the fore one more time. In the spring of 2010 the 1979 library was being demolished. Beulah Rose Hutchens reported that she and some of the other women who fought hard for its being built gathered at the place of destruction and were inspired to ask to man in charge if it would be possible to have some of the glazed bricks from the face of the building. He said he would collect fifty of them and they could pick them up at the building manager's office later in the week. Joyfully they returned, but to find that each facing brick, eight inches by eight inches in size weighed about fifty pounds. This was more than they bargained for. And first of all, there had to be a plan approved as to where a memorial would be placed. But the indomitable president of Reading Room, Marilyn Obermiller, went to the mayor of St. Cloud, Dave Kleis, and told him the story of the Reading Room from the beginning, probably back to 1865. At any rate, he said it would be done. But rather than placing the memorial on the grounds of the new 2008 library, the bricks would be laid into the entrance floor of the new addition to the Civic Center which is being built on the site of the old library. It would commemorate the Reading Room Society history that had been so prominently engaged in the growth of the city's library system from its beginning.

Joan Friebe, Helen Cotton, and Pat Honer in their thirties hats and furs at the Christmas at Whitney House party.

At the opening meeting of the Reading Room in 2009-2010, newly elected President Obermiller moved immediately into the momentum of interest that was growing in the history and in the future of the St. Cloud Reading Room Society. She opened the 2009-2010 fall meeting with the theme for the year, "Honoring Tradi-

Two past presidents, Ann Didier, 1990-1992 and Barbara Saigo, 2007-2009.

tion—Accepting Transition." She began each meeting of the year with a clever and interesting way of introducing the present members to the earliest members of the Society. She read short excerpts from accounts of activities and work being done over the years. Many of these came as a surprise to most members in attendance.

In the fall of 2009, one of the Society's speakers was Alexander Ames, a graduate student at St. Cloud State University who is writing his thesis on the "public memory of a local family and the construction

"Whitney" Christmas meeting. Patty Cummings, co-hostess Corrine Janochoski, Joan Kowalkowski.

Alex Ames presented the program and Jean Leighton co-hosted the "Whitney" Christmas meeting.

of a community." His work describes the important role played by a particular family. The family he chose to write about was typical of many who shaped St. Cloud from the last quarter of the nineteenth century. It was that of Albert G. Whitney and his wife, Alice Wheelock, who, as already noted in Chapter Four, came to Minnesota in the 1890s and played important roles in the business, social and educational development of St. Cloud from that time until their deaths. They left their indelible marks on the community far into the future. Their children and grandchildren, who moved to Minneapolis and other places, have continued to support the Whitney presence in St. Cloud.

The memory of these remarkable leaders and especially the time in which they lived in their family home—which is now surrounded by the campus of St. Cloud State University—was presented in a short play written by Alex Ames. Ames and members Jean Leighten and Corrine Janochoski, hosted the group who came dressed and hatted in clothes of the 1920s and 1930s. Music was provided by Ames at his harp, and he was joined by other State University students.

A Night Given to the Past, Reading Room Looks Forward

WITH PRIDE NOW IN THE opening of a new state-of-the-art library, looking into the future, the Reading Room Society envisions a whole new relationship between the Society and Library Board, the director and staff.

It looks forward to the many opportunities that will arise for them to be of service in responding to the cultural life needs of the community. They also look forward to the day they have met the

$15,000 goal to pay their pledge to the library, for a meeting room with a "St. Cloud Reading Room Society" plaque on its door

The year 2007 marked one hundred twenty-five years since the incorporation of the Reading Room Society. The great festivities of the new library opening over-shadowed Society plans for celebration, but the Society began a search into its past with an ad hoc committee by the History Committee Chair, Yvonne Schilplin. She approached Patricia Witte who accepted the challenge—on a volunteer basis—to write a history of the Society; she began her research in the spring of 2008. Happily, she found that the women of the Society had been very diligent in their record keeping, and scrapbooks provided more material than could be used. She and committee members searched through the boxes of records stored at the Stearns County History Museum Archives for pictures, noteworthy newspaper articles, minutes of meetings back to the very beginning. From all of this, as well as the carefully archived materials in the Stearns History Museum and Research Center, Witte was able to bring forth this book.

At the Annual Meeting of the St. Cloud Reading Room, May 13, 2010, President Marilyn Obermiller, after the regular reports, announced her hopes of a plan for signing up for committees for the coming year. She was working toward the idea of engaging the Reading Room membership in committees that would fulfill members' interests and needs, and which might even use the skills of members to offer programs for the meetings. She offered a form for the women to fill out that asked members to name subjects of particular interest to them. They were also to give areas of interest they are engaged in now or have been engaged in such as hobbies, work, travels, places they have lived, clubs they belong to or other interests.

The past committees that have been named for many years, and the special committees which have developed in the last two years, were also listed, along with a Vision Committee (for brain-storming of new directions and ideas for Reading Room.)

Then, she introduced Pat Witte, who, based on the research for the book and the directions suggested, presented her conclusions on WHO WE WERE; WHO WE ARE; WHAT NEXT?

"For the past two years we have been 'living with' the women who founded the Reading Room Society, some 130 years ago, and about those who carried it forward. I have been impressed; I have actually stood in awe of them. Yes, they were impressive in their idealism and the difficult community-building things they accomplished. Intellectually and physically they were unparalleled. They never made plans without figuring out a way to pay for them. They had from the beginning decided to have the money they made invested to generate more money.

"They had goals they never set aside. They were organized with the principles of working toward a free reading room and public library in the city of St. Cloud. No less important was their striving for intellectual improvement, and socialization among the members.

"We have lived in the era when that first and main goal has been reached many times over with the beautiful new library building and its state-of-the-art book and educational materials, with a very efficient lending system throughout a six-county area. Our primary goal has been fulfilled. So . . . what is next?

"We can't call in the ladies of the past to consult; we can't even try to emulate them or their world. But we can learn from their wisdom that has been passed along through succeeding generations of Reading Room members. We can't copy them because many of their ways have become obsolete. Many circumstances must be faced and dealt with before Reading Room can find itself on firm footing going into the future. The history of the Society will provide a great foundation, inspiration, but what a different world we live in!

"The role of women has changed dramatically. The well-educated woman is no longer primarily the daughter of a wealthy family. Women have professional and business associations outside of their regular work. Responsibilities with family and home, school and church, neighborhoods, all lay claim to their time. They become very selective in their choices of outside activities. It should be pointed out that people in their eighties are about the last vestige of a movement known as 'volunteerism'—they were free during the hours their children were in school and their husbands at work. That is not to belittle their work. Many took on 'professional' jobs, part time, unpaid. Most simply threw themselves into groups that did meaningful work and they worked hard to support goals of those organizations by organizing benefits and other ways of raising money for their support and becoming expert on the way.

"Reading Room is an organization of committees. They were instituted along the organizational plan of the General Federation of Women's Clubs and served well for many years. The committees studied aspects of the civic landscape that needed to be changed—and then went to work, physically, planting flowers and trees in designated park areas. Through efforts of getting people to clean up their yards and surrounding areas they convinced the city of the need for garbage removal. They saw the problems and acted with dramatic gestures that pointed them out and influenced the town leaders and citizens for change. These women were 'volunteers'; they were 'activists' without marches, without signs and shouting.

"The Reading Room Society did not fear change, nor shy away from it. When we see the tremendous work and money and responsibility they gave to the Carnegie Library that was built in 1902, it might be expected that they would fight its replacement. No, they moved on and led a fifteen year fight to replace it. It was a hard fight through the 1960s and 1970s. It took four bond issue votes to finally pass a bill to build a new library. That new library in 1974 might have been considered certain fulfillment of Reading Room's goal, but the NEW new library in 2008 has finally impressed many of Reading Room members that they were good friends and supporters of the library for 125 years. But the library no longer depended on Reading Room.

"Now! We face change in organizational structure and the emphasis we decide to place on the work we do. We have two outstanding goals at the present time. First, we have a commitment to raise enough money to pay our pledge to acquire the room we will call "Reading Room Society" at the new library. Second, we have to raise money to publish the history of the Society in the coming year.

"Then, we are inheritors of a committee structure that does not seem to fit the interests or needs of the members. We continue to ask people to sign up for committees for which it appears they have no interest. What is interesting to our members? Let's ask them. We have a great group of women who are leaders in the community; educated women who have professions they work at; and women who are artists, activists, teachers, leaders in community organizations, scientists, master gardeners, and on and on. Let's hear from them. Let's hear from all of us! For many years, the speakers were the committee members themselves who prepared talks about a subject of interest to the committee, and delivered to the members. Those were the programs. We could use the 'Program time' at some meetings to discuss these ideas.

"This is a time to reconsider the second goal of our tradition, one that is a lifetime work—intellectual growth. Let's find ways to use the great gifts that are right here among us. But first, let's have open discussion about the questions—really open—to let it be known what is desired from the Society. New members, younger members must speak up. You women, especially, must be a little tired of hearing about the women of the past. They were great, did great things for their time, but they couldn't hold a candle to the women gathered here!"

The last meeting of 2009-2010 was held at the St. Cloud Country Club, the location for most of the meetings. The speakers brought a light note for an early summer program on container gardening by a local master gardener. Also, from the library came news that soon there will be electronic books to borrow. The librarian passed some e-books around as she described their use and members got a "hands on" experience of the "books" of our immediate future. It was a wrap-up meeting that observed the old art of flower gardening and the new experience of e-book reading.

After a lovely and lively dinner the president met with people who had signed up for the Program Committee for next year to try to start up and activate new ideas for programming. They will look into the areas that interested the women of today, from their personal interests and training to wide ranging problems that face us in this area of the world So, poised to move on by President Obermiller's enthusiasm and ideas for the future in her second term in office, it appears that St. Cloud Reading Room Society is going to move ahead with a whole new spirit. With ideas from the members that came in response to the questionnaire, there will be more discussion about what the group's wishes showing creativity in their ideas breathing new life into an old organization in this world of beauty—and chaos.

We have wound up one hundred thirty years since that memorable meeting of forty women at the house of Helen Moore against a theme: "Let us honor tradition, while accepting transition, and let us envision the future."

And we will start the one hundred thirty-first with a goal: "Let us expand our horizons through involvement in areas of literacy, civic affairs, education, and improvement of women's lives." Marilyn Obermiller 1909 to 1910.

Past Presidents

1880 – 1881   Mrs. H.C. Waite
1881 – 1882   Mrs. H.C. Waite
1882 – 1883   Mrs. L.W. Collins
1883 – 1884   Mrs. J.E. West
1884 – 1885   Mrs. L.A. Evans
1885 – 1886   Mrs. J.E. West
1886 – 1887   Mrs. L.W. Collins
1887 – 1888   Mrs. C.A. Gilman
1888 – 1889   Mrs. C.A. Gilman
1889 – 1890   Mrs. C.A. Gilman
1890 – 1891   Mrs. L.W. Collins
1891 – 1892   Mrs. George W. Stewart
1892 – 1893   Mrs. George W. Stewart
1893 – 1894   Mrs. A.L. Tileston
1894 – 1895   Mrs. A. Barto
1895 – 1896   Mrs. A. Barto
1896 – 1897   Miss Mary M. Campbell
1897 – 1898   Mrs. J.E. West
1898 – 1899   Mrs. Thomas Foley
1899 – 1900   Mrs. W.B. Mitchell (February to September)

1900 – 1901	Mrs. Alvah Eastman
1901 – 1902	Mrs. Alvah Eastman
1902 – 1903	Mrs. C.A. Cooper
1903 – 1904	Mrs. C.A. Cooper
1904 – 1905	Mrs. J.E. Jenks
1905 - 1906	Mrs. C.L. Atwood
1906 – 1907	Mrs. C.L. Atwood
1907 - 1908	Mrs. W.W. Smith
1908 – 1909	Mrs. W.W. Smith
1909 - 1910	Mrs. J.E. Jenks
1910 – 1911	Mrs. E.F. Moore
1911 – 1912	Mrs. E.F. Moore
1912 – 1913	Mrs. Frederick Schilplin (Maude)
1913 – 1914	Mrs. Frederick Schilplin
1914 – 1915	Mrs. Alois Tschumperlin
1915 – 1916	Mrs. Alois Tschumperlin
1916 – 1917	Mrs. W.W. Smith
1917 – 1918	Mrs. W.W. Smith
1918 – 1919	Mrs. A.G. Whitney
1919 – 1920	Mrs. H.R. Neide
1920 – 1921	Mrs. H.R. Neide
1921 – 1922	Mrs. J.C. Brown
1922 – 1923	Mrs. J.C. Brown
1923 – 1924	Mrs. C.C. Dragoo
1924 – 1925	Mrs. C.C. Dragoo
1925 – 1926	Mrs. Wm. Sartell
1926 – 1927	Mrs. Wm. Sartell
1927 – 1928	Mrs. H.C. Bowing
1928 - 1929	Mrs. H.C. Bowing
1930 - 1931	Mrs. A.L. Riley
1931 – 1932	Mrs. C.B. Lewis
1932 - 1933	Mrs. C.B. Lewis
1933 – 1934	Mrs. C.E. Vasaly
1934 – 1935	Mrs. George Selke

1935 – 1936	Mrs. C.S. Olds
1936 – 1937	Mrs. C.S. Olds
1937 – 1938	Mrs. Allen A. Atwood
1938 – 1939	Mrs. Allen A. Atwood
1939 – 1940	Mrs. L.H. Rice
1940 – 1941	Mrs. L.H. Rice
1941 – 1942	Mrs. Leslie Zeleny
1942 – 1943	Mrs. William Freeman
1943 – 1944	Mrs. H.B. Gough
1944 – 1945	Mrs. H.B. Gough
1945 – 1946	Mrs. J.M. Dobson
1946 – 1947	Mrs. J.M. Dobson
1947 – 1948	Mrs. F.E. Perkins
1948 – 1949	Mrs. F.E. Perkins
1949 – 1950	Mrs. M.J. Daboll
1950 – 1951	Mrs. C.B. Lewis
1951 – 1952	Mrs. Colie Guy
1952 – 1953	Mrs. Colie Guy
1953 – 1954	Mrs. John Goven
1954 – 1955	Mrs. John Goven
1955 – 1956	Mrs. W.B. Richards
1956 – 1957	Mrs. W.B. Richards
1957 – 1958	Mrs. C.H. Richter
1958 – 1959	Mrs. Charles Richter
1959 – 1960	Mrs. Kurt Stai
1960 – 1961	Mrs. Kurt Stai
1961 – 1962	Mrs. Frank Murphy
1962 – 1963	Mrs. Frank Murphy
1963 – 1964	Mrs. Thomas Donlin
1964 – 1965	Mrs. J.C. Laughlin
1965 – 1966	Mrs. J.C. Laughlin
1966 – 1967	Mrs. A.P. Baston
1967 – 1968	Mrs. A.P. Baston
1968 – 1969	Miss Ruth M. Moscrip

1969 – 1970   Miss Ruth M. Moscrip
1970 – 1971   Mrs. Howard Russell
1971 – 1972   Mrs. Howard Russell
1972 – 1973   Mrs. Robert T. Peterson
1973 – 1974   Mrs. Robert T. Peterson
1974 – 1975   Mrs. Max Landy
1975 – 1976   Mrs. Max Landy
1976 – 1977   Mrs. Leigh Rethmeier
1977 – 1978   Mrs. Leigh Rethmeier
1978 – 1979   Mrs. B. Howard Flanagan
1979 – 1980   Mrs. B. Howard Flanagan (Gen)
1980 – 1981   Miss Mary C. Baker
1981 – 1982   Mrs. B. Howard Flanagan (Genevieve)
1982 – 1983   Mrs. John Benson (Helen)
1983 – 1984   Mrs. John Benson (Helen)
1984 – 1985   Mrs. Frances Voelker (Mil)
1985 – 1986   Mrs. Frances Voelker
1986 – 1987   Mrs. Warren Hutchens (Beulah Rose)
1987 – 1988   Mrs. Warren Hutchens
1988 – 1989   Mrs. Glen Carlson (Blanche)
1989 – 1990   Mrs. Glen Carlson
1990 – 1991   Mrs. Alex Didier (Ann)
1991 – 1992   Mrs. Ann Didier
1992 – 1993   Mrs. Helen Jones
1993 – 1994   Mrs. Helen Jones
1994 – 1995   Margaret Kline
1995 – 1996   Margaret Kline
1996 – 1997   Rachel Veeser
1997 – 1998   Rachel Veeser
1998 – 1999   Yvonne Schilplin
1999 – 2000   Yvonne Schilplin
2000 – 2001   Karen Vann
2001 – 2002   Karen Vann
2002 – 2003   Judy Rothstein

2003 – 2004   Joan Teigen
2004 – 2005   Pat Christianson
2005 – 2006   M. Constance Crane
2006 – 2007   M. Constance Crane
2007 – 2008   Barbara Saigo
2008 – 2009   Barbara Saigo
2009 – 2010   Marilyn Obermiller

Bibliography

Dominick, John J. *The Triplet City*: Produced Association with the St.Cloud Area Chamber of Commerce: Windsor Publications, Inc. Woodland Hills, California, 1983.*

Mitchel, William B.: *History of Stearns County*, Volume I and II: Published in 1915.

Rowland, Ph.D., Howard Ray; *Loyal to Thy Fine Tradition; St. Cloud State University -125 Years In Words and Pictures-1869-1994*. Published in 1994 by Donning Co. Publishers, Virginia Beach, Virginia 23462.

Many quotations from the newspapers of St. Cloud were used. They were acknowledged within the narrative throughout the book, unless from time to time there would be a story in the archives that had been cut out and preserved but without the date and/or sometimes the newspaper source. These had to be guessed according to the story itself and put into context.

William Mitchell's *History of Stearns County*. Mitchell gave a wonderful detailed account of the beginnings and the work and growth of the Society until 1915 when his book was published.

Clara Donlin's *Profile of a Library*: A short unpublished history of the Reading Room from its beginnings until the opening of the

Carnegie Library. It was Mrs. Donlin, who, to the best of the author's knowledge, coined the apt expression, "Indomitable Ladies" in reference to Reading Room Society members. I felt I should give recognition to her for my use in the title of this book.

PKW

Index

About the Author

Pat Witte and her husband, Bob, came to the area from Minneapolis and Edina where they had lived until then, spent their lives and raised their two sons. In 1974, they built a country home in 50 acres of woods on the Clearwater River, but after twenty years, they decided to move into town. They chose St. Cloud because they had many friends and associations, and found St. Cloud a good place to call home.

Pat is a graduate of Washburn High School, Minneapolis, and of St. Benedict's College, St. Joseph. Among the many church activities over their 62 years of marriage, some were involved with writing. She wrote the history of St. Marcus Parish, Clear Lake where she and Bob were members, and most recently, the 150th Anniversary Book of St. Mary's Cathedral—*St. Mary's Parish: 150 years*—in 2004. In 2008 she was asked to write the History of Reading Room - and found inspiration in the women who over more than 130 years worked tirelessly to see that St. Cloud had a library. They more than achieved that goal. Pat says she will lay down her pen at this point; that is, turn off her computer.